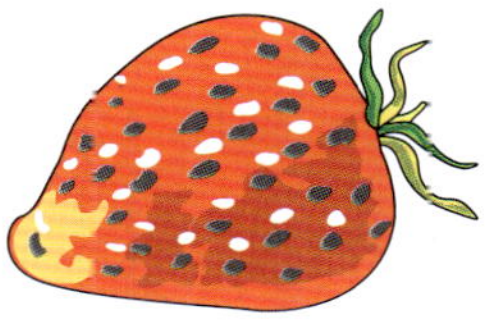

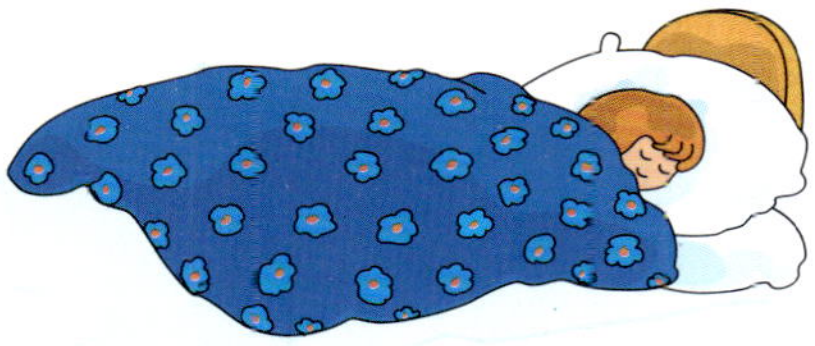

This picture dictionary is an interesting and enjoyable way of introducing any young reader to words in everyday use – words that need to become part of the modern child's growing vocabulary.

The use of colourful, fun pictures accompanied by simply constructed sentences will delight any young reader and will, at the same time, help them to recognise, learn and remember a variety of different words.

A humorous and light-hearted approach has been used in both the illustrations and the text. We hope that this will capture children's interest and stimulate their desire to read and develop their skills in writing and spelling. This is a book to dip into again and again to really learn a lot about words, or simply have fun.

Written by Anne McKie
Illustrated by Q2solutions

4 North Parade, Bath, BA1 1LF, UK.
Printed in China.

THE FUN-TO-LEARN

PICTURE DICTIONARY

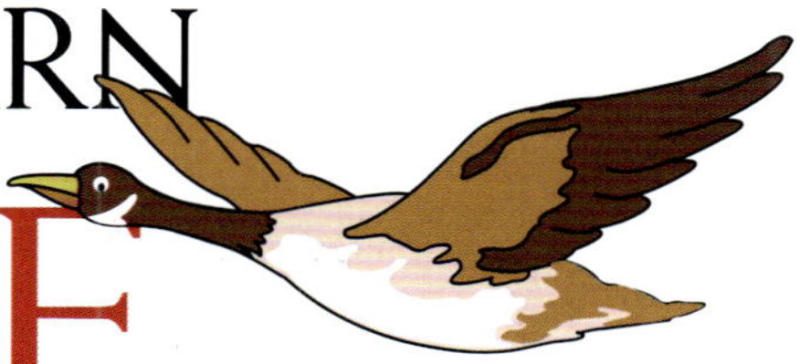

More than 1300 words explained
together with 850 colour illustrations

A a

able
If you are able to do something – you can do it. I am able to read this dictionary, are you?

above
The sky is above the land. Above is opposite to below. The land is below the sky.

accident
An accident happens by chance and is always unexpected.

acrobats
Acrobats are very good at balancing tricks. You can see them performing on stage or in the circus.

across
When you walk across the road, you cross from one side to the other. Take care!

address
Your address is where you live. Write clearly when you address an envelope. This helps the postman deliver it to the correct address.

adult
An adult is a grown-up, not a child.

advertisement
An advertisement tells you about something for sale. 'Ads' are often seen on television, in newspapers and sometimes on the side of a bus.

aeroplane
A machine with wings that travels through the air, flown by a pilot. It is often called a 'plane'.

afraid
When you feel afraid, you are frightened.

after
1. After can mean later on. Will you wash-up after tea?
2. It can also mean following behind. The fox ran after the goose.

again
To do something once more. Do your homework again!

against
1. He was standing against the tins. He was next to them.
2. It can mean opposed to. Tom is against washing!

age
How many years have you lived? This is your age.

agree
To think the same as other people. We all agree your hat is too big.

ahead
Ahead means in front of. Go ahead and I'll follow.

air
Air is all around. It is a mixture of gases we must breathe to live.

airport
The place where aircrafts take off and land with cargo and passengers.

alarm
An alarm attracts attention. It is often a warning signal.

alike
Things that look or are the same.

alone
No one is with me. I'm all alone.

alphabet
Here are the twenty-six letters of the alphabet.

alive
Animals, plants and people are all alive. They are living things.

all
All the mice are washing-up. That means every one of them.

allow
Allow is to let someone do something. Are you allowed to do that?

also
Also means as well. I have a hamster, also a gold fish.

aircraft
The name for different kinds of machines that fly.

always
The same at all times. The sun always rises in the morning.

ambulance
Sick or injured people are rushed to hospital in an ambulance.

an
You use this tiny word instead of a, when the word begins with a, e, i, o, or u.

and
And joins words together. Jill and John and Mary are pulling faces.

angry
If you are angry you feel very cross about something.

annoy
To make someone cross or tease them. John was beginning to annoy his dad.

another
Tell me another story means tell me one more.

answer
When we are asked a question, we must give an answer or reply.

any
Any can mean some, every or even one. It is often fixed in front of other words.

anyone
Is there anyone there?

anything
Have you anything to tell me?

anywhere
I can't find my glasses anywhere!

appetite
When you really want a meal and your dinner smells lovely, it gives you an appetite.

apron
An apron tied round you protects you from getting in a mess.

aquarium
A glass tank full of water for plants and fish.

archer
Someone who shoots arrows from a bow. It is called archery.

area
The area is the size of a space or surface.

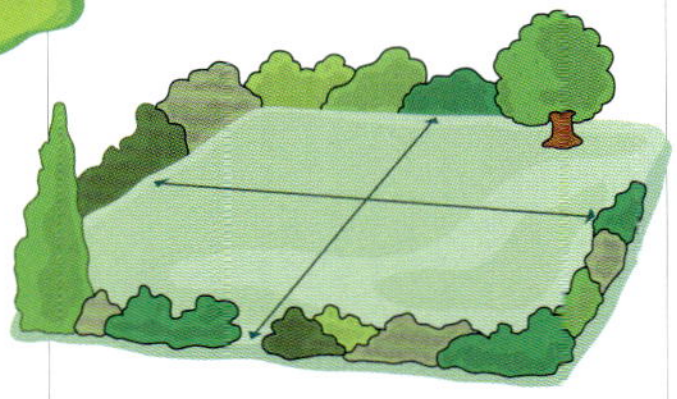

arithmetic
Using numbers to add, subtract, multiply and divide.

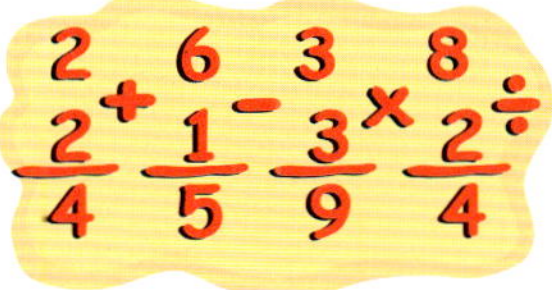

around
How would you like to fly around the world?

arrive
To reach a place is to arrive. The bus will arrive at ten o'clock.

artist
Famous artists produce works of art when they draw and paint.

ask
Do you want to know something? Then just ask!

asleep
Grandad is asleep in his chair. Soon he will be awake.

astronaut
An astronaut is a person who travels in space.

athlete
A person who trains hard to be good at sports and games.

atlas
A book full of maps.

attack
Attack is to begin to fight.

awake
I can't sleep, I am still wide awake!

away
The baby birds have flown away. They are no longer here.

author
An author writes books, plays and stories.

autumn
The season after summer and before winter when crops are harvested.

B b

baby
A baby is a very young child.

back
1. Back means behind, opposite to front. Go to the back of the queue!
2. I fell off the stool and hurt my back.

animal
Every living creature is an animal

B b

backwards
When you are on a swing, you swing to the back then move to the front.

bad
Bad means not good. Uncle is in a bad mood; he has a bad cold.

badge
Badges are worn by soldiers, scouts and members of clubs. Do you collect badges?

bag
Bags are containers for holding things and carrying them around.

bake
To cook food in a hot oven. The baker bakes bread and cakes.

balance
To hold something or yourself quite steady.

balloon
Balloons float when blown up, because they are filled with air.

bank
I. A mound of earth, a river-bank or sand-bank.

2. A building where your money is safely locked away.

barbecue
Cooking out of doors.

bare
If you are bare, you have nothing on. If the cupboard is bare, there is nothing in it.

bark
1. The noise made by a dog. Woof, woof!
2. The rough skin covering a tree.

barn
A farm building used for storage.

barrel
A large wooden tub to store food and drink.

base
The bottom of something. The part on which it stands.

baseball
A favourite American team-game like rounders.

bath
You can put your whole self in the bath. Remember to wash behind your ears!

battery
A battery stores small amounts of electricity. All these things run on batteries.

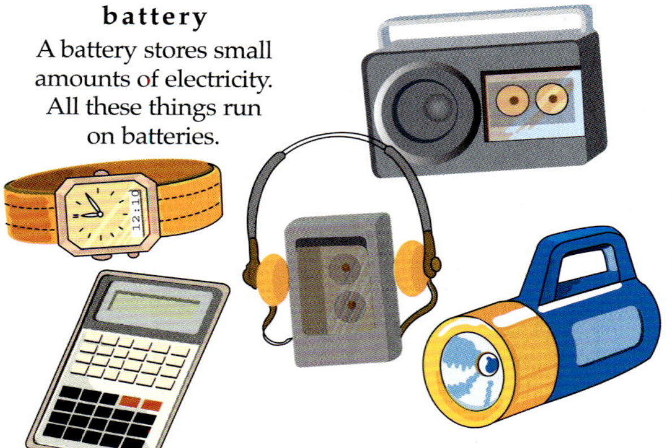

beach
The beach is the strip of sand at the edge of the sea.

bead
A little ball with a hole pierced through. You thread beads on a string to make a necklace.

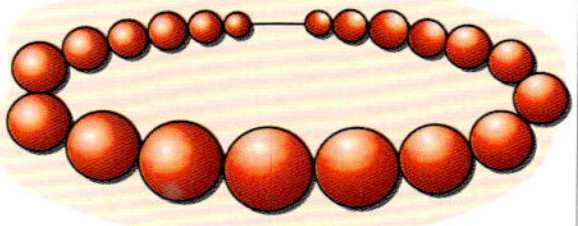

beak
A bird's bill or mouth. They all look very different.

beard
Hair that grows on a man's face and chin.

beat
1. Beat is to hit over and over again.
2. It can also mean to win. I can beat you at tennis!

beautiful
Things that are lovely to look at or listen to are beautiful.

because
My cousin is angry because a rabbit has eaten all his plants.

bed
At night we go to sleep on a bed.

before
1. Before means earlier. The tortoise arrived before the hare.

2. It can mean in front of. Who is standing before the drawbridge?

begin
To begin with is another way of saying to start with. Begin the book at the beginning!

believe
Do you believe in stories about fairies? Do you think they are true?

bell
There are many different kinds of bells. They make a ringing noise.

below
Below means underneath. A mole digs tunnels below the ground.

belt
A thin strip of leather or plastic fastened round your waist.

bend
1. A curve in the road is called a bend.
2. A strong man can bend an iron bar.

beneath
Another word for lower than. The earth is beneath the sky.

berry
Small juicy fruits with seeds. Some are good to eat, some are poisonous.

best
Susan's cake is best. It is better than all the rest.

between
In the middle of two things.

beyond
The rainbow is beyond the hills. It is far away, out of reach.

bicycle
A bike has two wheels and is pedalled along by the rider.

big
An elephant is big, but a whale is bigger. It is the biggest mammal in the world.

billiards
A game played on a special table with balls and cues.

binoculars
A telescope made with two eyes. Binoculars make things seem nearer.

bite
To bite is to cut into something with your teeth.

bitter
Bitter tastes sharp. A lemon is bitter.

blackboard
Every school has a blackboard. You write on it with chalk.

blanket
A soft warm cover. In winter you snuggle under the blankets.

blizzard
A blinding storm with wind and driving snow.

blood
Red liquid in your veins. Cut a finger and it bleeds.

blossom

A flower is a blossom. Some blossom comes before fruit; apple, pear and cherry blossom.

boat
A boat floats on water. Some have sails and oars, others have engines.

body
The whole of you is your body.

boil
When water is heated it bubbles up and boils. The kettle's boiling!

bone
Your skeleton is made up of all the bones inside your body.

bird
All birds have wings and feathers and most of them can fly.

birthday
Your birthday is the day you were born.

biscuit
A crunchy flat kind of cake. Yum! Yum!

bit
A little piece or fragment of a bigger thing.

blow
1. Blow is to make the air move. The wind blows.
2. It can mean a smack or a hard knock.

blush
When you blush your face turns pink.

bonfire
You light a bonfire outside in the garden.

book
A book is a collection of sheets of paper bound together. Usually a book contains words and pictures.

boomerang
An Australian weapon like a curved stick. When you throw it, it comes back.

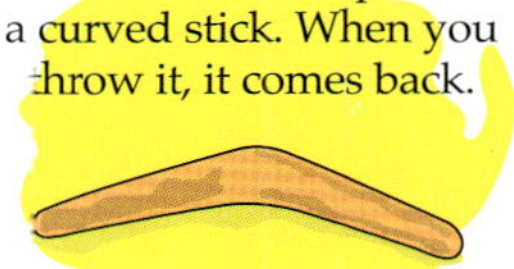

borrow
To ask someone for something for a little while. Can I borrow your tie?

bottle
A container for holding liquids. You can pour easily from a bottle.

bottom
The lowest part of something. The treasure is at the bottom of the sea.

bounce
When you bounce you spring up and down again and again.

bouquet
A bunch of flowers nicely wrapped.

bow
1. There's a bow of ribbon round the box.

2. When you bend over from the waist you bow.

3. Robin Hood shot arrows from a bow.

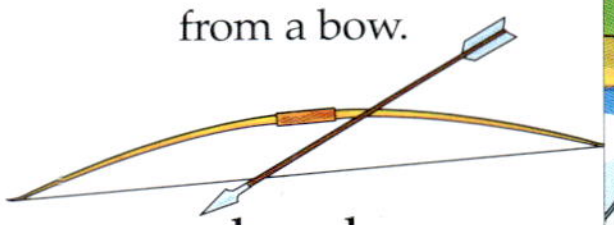

bowl
A hollow, deep dish like a shallow basin.

boy
A boy is a young, male child who will grow up to be a man.

bracelet
A piece of jewellery worn round your wrist.

branch
The branches are the arms of a tree; they spread out from the trunk.

bread
Bread is made of flour, water and yeast, left to rise, then baked in the oven.

break
1. Break is to smash to pieces.
2. It can also mean a pause. Take a break!

breath
Breath is the air you draw in and blow out of your lungs.

brick
A block of clay that has been baked, then used to build walls.

bridge
A bridge is a way built over a gap so people can cross.

bright
Ben is sitting in the bright sun in his bright yellow shorts.

bring
Bring is to fetch or carry back. The opposite of take. Bring me my supper!

broken
My leg is broken. I must be careful not to break the other one.

broom
A long-handled sweeping brush.

brought
When the giant shouted for his supper, his wife brought it at once.

brush
A handle with hairs or bristles. What a lot of brushes we all use!

bubble
A transparent ball of liquid, filled with gas and air, that floats.

bucket
You can fill a bucket with water and carry it.

bud
A flower or leaf before it opens.

budgerigar
A cage bird and favourite pet. You can teach some to speak very well.

build
To build is to make something by putting several things together.

bulb
1. An electric light bulb lights up when it is switched on.
2. A flower bulb grows below the soil and flowers in spring.

bulldozer
A big earthmoving tractor with a blade at the front.

bump
When you knock or jolt something you bump it.

bungalow
A house with all the rooms on one floor.

bunk
A bunk is a bed in a ship's cabin. Have you ever slept in bunk beds?

burglar
Someone who breaks into your house to steal things.

burn
If you set fire to paper it will burn. Be careful not to burn your fingers.

burst
Prick a balloon with a pin and it will burst.

bus
A bus carries lots of passengers around. Some buses are double-deckers. You go upstairs to the top deck.

bush
A small tree or shrub, like a rose bush.

butcher
A man who cuts meat into pieces to sell for cooking.

butter
Cream is churned or whipped until it thickens into butter.

buy
To buy is to pay money for something. Once you have bought it, it is yours.

calculator
A machine that fits into your pocket. It can add, subtract, divide and multiply.

calendar
A calendar shows you the days and dates in each month of the year.

call
This word can mean lots of things.
"I am going to call my baby Sophie."
"Call round at my house."
"I must make a phone call."
"Call out if you need me."

canoe
A light, narrow boat you sit inside and paddle.

capital
1. A large letter of the alphabet.
2. A capital city is the main city of a country.

captain
1. The captain is in charge of a ship.
2. The team captain is the leader of the team.

C c

cab
You take a cab in America, a taxi in London. You pay the driver for a ride.

cactus
A prickly desert plant.

cage
Animals and birds are often kept in a cage. Bars on the sides keep them in.

cake
Make a cake, then bake a cake. This is a birthday cake.

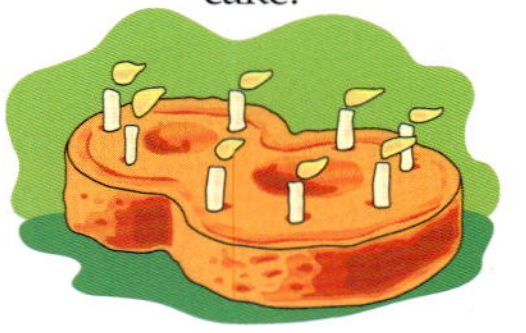

camera
A machine for taking photographs.

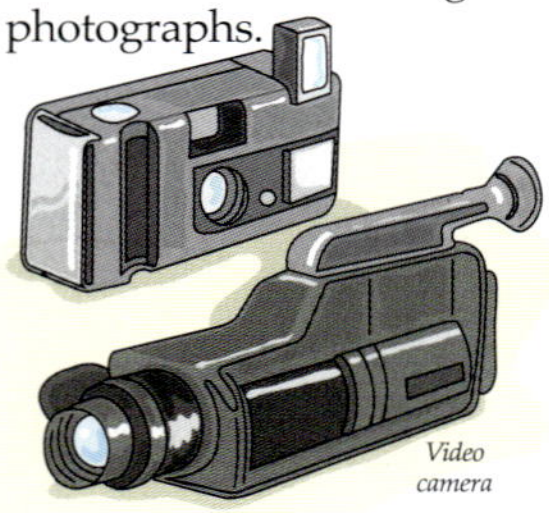

camp
You camp out of doors in a tent on a campsite.

candle
A stick of wax with a wick down the middle. It burns when you light it.

cannon
A very big gun.

Some cannons are mounted on wheels.

car
A motor vehicle with an engine and four wheels used to carry people.

card
A stiff piece of paper with lots of uses.

carpet
A deep, soft material covering the bare floor.

carry
The waiter carried the tray. He took it from one place to another.

cartoon
A funny drawing or a short film made with comic characters.

cassette
A small flat box that contains the tape for a video or tape recorder.

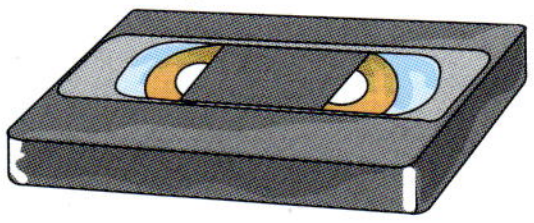

castle
A home for kings and noblemen, with thick, stone towers to keep their enemies out.

caterpillar
A grub which becomes a pupa, then turns into a butterfly or moth.

cattle
Some cattle are wild like bison and buffalo. Others are domesticated like our cows.

ceiling
This is the top of a room, the floor is the bottom.

cellar
A room under the house.

centimetre
One hundred centimetres equal one metre.

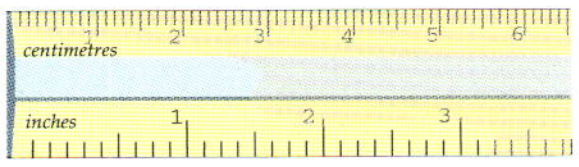

centre
The middle of something.

century
A century is one hundred years.

cereal
Maize, barley, rice, wheat and oats are all cereals.

certain
To be certain is to be sure. I am sure four comes before five!

chain
Rings linked together in a row.

chair
A seat for one person. Baby Bear had a tiny chair.

champion
Champion is another word for winner.

chance
1. It happened by chance means just by luck.
2. Give me a chance to win!

change
To make something different. He changed his hairstyle.

chase
The goose is chasing the hen, then the duck joins in the chase.

cheap
Cheap things cost less money.

cheer
To shout and make a noise when your team is winning.

cheese
A food made from milk. It has a savoury taste and is good for you.

chemist
Someone who makes up medicines.

chest
1. A strong box.
2. You puff out your chest when you take a deep breath.

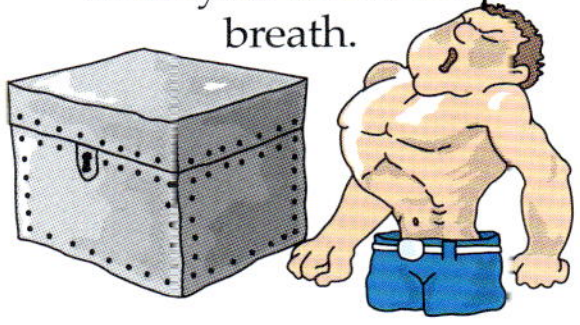

chief
Chief means leader. It can also mean the most important.

child
A child is a young boy or girl. Fred and Freda are children.

chimney
A chimney takes the smoke away from the fire.

chocolate
A hot drink or a variety of delicious sweets.

choir
A group of singers, often singing hymns in church.

choose
Choose is to pick. Can you choose the biggest ice cream?

chop
Chop means to cut into pieces or to cut down.

Christmas
This is the time that people celebrate the birth of Jesus.

church
People pray and worship in a building called a church.

cinema
A large building where films are shown to the public.

circle
A perfectly round figure like a ring.

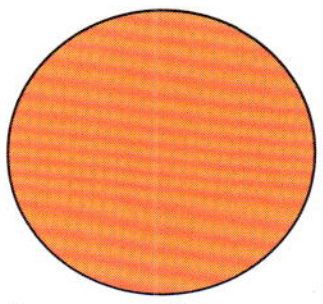

circumference
The distance round a circle.

circus
A travelling show with clowns, animals and acrobats.

city
A very large town is called a city.

clap
To strike your hands together. When an audience claps it is called applause.

class
A group of people learning things together.

classroom
A room where the class meets for lessons.

clay
Wet, soft, sticky earth that is made into pots or bricks and baked hard.

clean
Clean is well washed and not dirty at all.

cliff
A cliff is a steep rockface. Do not go near the edge!

climate
The different kinds of weather in all sorts of places.

clock
An instrument that measures and tells us the time.

close

1. Close means to shut. Close that window, I'm in a draught!

2. It can also mean near. Sit close by me, I feel lonely!

clothes

All sorts of different things to wear made of cloth.

cloud

A cloud is made up of tiny drops of water floating together in the sky.

clumsy

A clumsy person is awkward, and bumps into things.

coach

1. A coach is a teacher or trainer.
2. It is also a bus or a railway carriage.

coal

A hard, black rock dug out of the ground. It makes a lovely fire.

coast

Where the land meets the sea.

cobweb

A spider spins a silken cobweb to trap insects.

coconut

A huge, hairy nut that grows high up in a palm tree.

coffee

Coffee beans are roasted and ground up. Add boiling water and you have a lovely cup of coffee.

coin

A piece of money made of metal.

cold

It is always cold in winter. Now is the time you catch a cold.

collar

A shirt collar fits round your neck. The dog has a collar round his neck too.

collect

Collect means to gather together.

colour

There are many colours, here are just a few.

come

To come means to move near and not go away.

comma

A comma is a punctuation mark. It divides two parts of a sentence.

compare

You notice if things are alike or different, you compare them.

compass

You can find your way if you have a compass. The needle always points north.

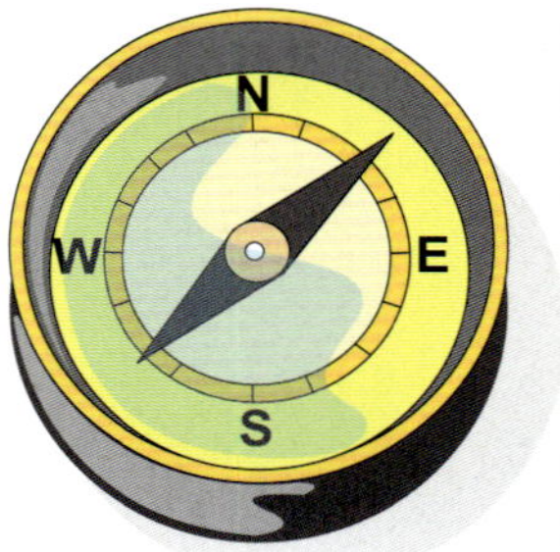

complete

Complete has nothing missing. This puzzle is complete.

computer

A machine that can store, process and give out large amounts of information at great speed.

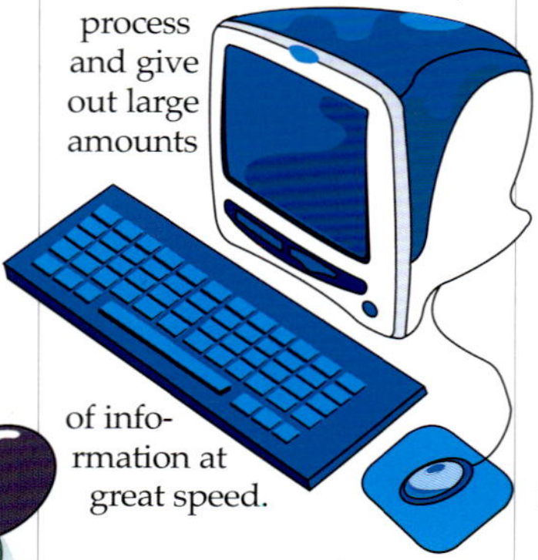

concert

A m usical entertainment given by an orchestra, band and sometimes a choir.

cone

A cone is round and flat at the bottom and goes to a point at the top.

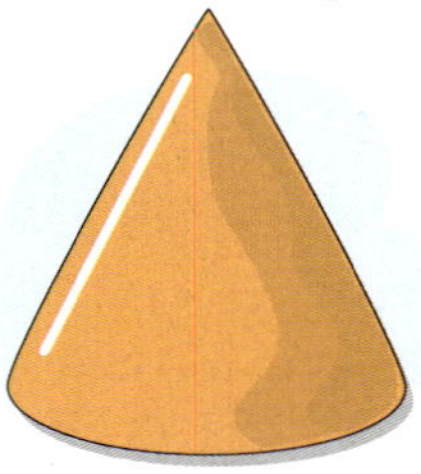

conjuror

A conjuror does magic tricks.

connect

Connect means to join together.

construct

Construct is to make or build. Boys love construction toys.

continent

A large mass of land. The Earth is made up of seas and continents.

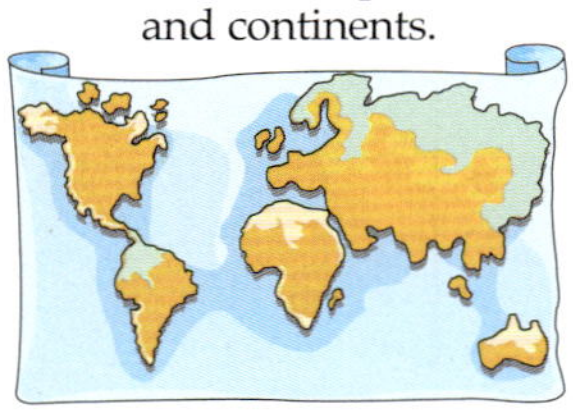

cook

A person that makes a meal ready to eat. I cooked the breakfast this morning!

cool

Cool feels a little bit warmer than cold. On a hot day the water feels cool.

copy

To make something that is exactly like another.

corner

A street comer is where two streets meet. Two straight lines meeting make a corner.

correct

Right, with no mistakes at all.

cosmonaut

A Russian spaceman.

costume

Putting on a costume means dressing up. In some countries national costume is worn.

cottage

A little house in the country. Here is a thatched cottage.

count

To count is to add up how many there are.

country

1. When you leave town and begin to see fields you are in the country.
2. A country is a land and all its people, America; Spain; China.

cover

"Cover me up in bed. I have such a pretty, blue cover."

cowboy

A man in charge of herds of cattle on a ranch.

crab

A crab is a sea creature with a hard shell and two claws like pincers.

crack

1. A sharp noise like the crack of thunder.
2. A very fine split. This cup is cracked!

cradle

A bed for a baby.

crash

1. A sudden fall which makes a loud noise.
2. An accident when people or things are smashed.

crawl

To move around on your hands and knees.

crayon
A coloured, wax stick for drawing pictures.

creature
All living things except plants.

crime
A wrong deed. This burglar has committed a crime.

cross
1. These lines re in the shape of a cross.

2. When we are cross we feel angry.
3. Cross the road with care.

crowd
Many people all together in one place.

crown
The head-dress of kings and queens, made of gold and jewels.

cry
1. When you cry, tears fall from your eyes.
2. When you cry for help, you shout loudly.

cube
A solid shape with six equal square sides.

curtain
Cloths that cover windows or make a screen on the front of a stage.

curve
A bent line that has no straight part.

cushion
A soft, fat pillow usually on a chair.

customer
A person who goes into a shop to buy something.

cut
To divide into pieces with scissors, a knife or a saw.

cycle
Another word for bicycle. I cycled through a puddle.

cylinder
A shape like a tube. It can be solid or hollow.

D d

daily
Daily is every day. The newspaper is delivered daily.

dairy
Milk is kept at the dairy. Often cheese, butter and yoghurt are made there.

damage
The storm caused a lot of damage, it did a lot of harm.

damp
Damp means slightly wet. Babies are sometimes damp!

dance
Dance is to move around to music. The waltz is a dance.

danger
Danger is something harmful. How very dangerous!

dark
Dark means no light. Witches go out on dark nights, dressed in dark clothes.

date
The date tells you the day, the month and the year.

daughter
The female child of her parents.

day
A day lasts twenty four hours. There are seven days in a week.

decide
If you make up your mind, you decide.

deck
The deck is the floor of a ship.

decorate
When you decorate a room for a party, you make it look pretty.

deep
Deep goes a long way down. In Switzerland the snow can be very deep.

delicatessen
A shop selling cooked meats and cheeses from different countries.

delicious
Something good to eat tastes delicious.

deliver
When the postman delivers the letters, he hands them over to you.

dentist
The dentist takes care of your teeth.

describe
To write or tell someone about something.

desert
A land where there is very little water and nothing can grow.

desk
A little table which sometimes has a sloping top. You sit at a desk to write and read.

detective
A person who tries to solve a crime.

detergent
We use all kinds of detergents when we are spring cleaning. They help dissolve the dirt.

diagram
A drawing or plan that helps explain things.

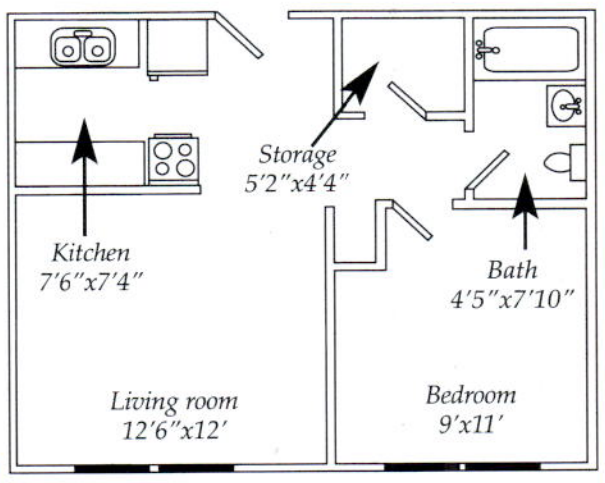

diamond
A very hard precious stone. It has to be cut and polished before it is made into jewellery.

diary
A daily record of events. You make notes in your diary as a reminder.

dictionary
A book that tells you the meaning of words.

different
Different means not the same. Can you spot the difference?

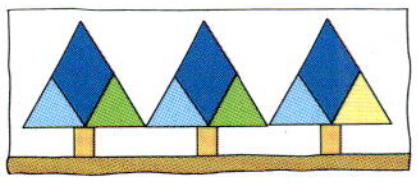

difficult
A difficult thing is hard to do, not easy.

dig
You dig the earth with a spade. A machine called a digger can dig deeper and faster.

dinosaur
These great reptiles lived on Earth millions of years ago. Now they are all gone.

direction
The way in which you go. You're going in the wrong direction!

dirty
If you need a wash, you are dirty.

disappear
If something has disappeared, it has vanished and can't be found.

discover
This means to find something. Christopher Columbus discovered America.

disguise
A disguise changes the look of something or somebody!

dish
A dish is a shallow bowl or plate like a pie dish.

distance
Distance is the space between two things or places.

dive
To jump or fall head first into something. You dive into the water and you make a dive for the ball.

do
Do is to carry out a thing. Busy people are doing things all day long!

doctor
A doctor looks after people who are ill.

dolphin
Dolphins are intelligent and playful creatures. They swim very fast in groups, then suddenly leap out of the water high into the air.

dome
A dome has a shape like half an orange. A dome is usually placed on top of a building.

door
To enter a room or building you have to go in by the door.

double
1. Double is twice as much.
2. Do you have a double? – someone who looks just like you.

down
Down means to go lower. Get down from that ladder!

dragon
Dragons can be found in fairy tales and legends.

draw
You use a pencil, a crayon or chalks to draw. Who drew that?

drawer
An open box that slides in and out of furniture.

dream
The thoughts that come into your head when you are asleep.

drink
To drink is to swallow a liquid. What would you like to drink?

drive
1. To drive is to make any vehicle travel along.
2. When the farmer drives his geese into the pens, he makes them go inside.

3. The drive is the road leading up to a house.

drop
1. To drop is to let something fall.
2. It also means a little blob of liquid.

drown
If you sink below the waves and breathe in water instead of air, you drown.

dry
Dry has no wet at all. Rub the baby dry, then hang the towel out to dry!

during
During the storm I hid under the bed. During means while it lasted.

dye
If you dye a garment or your hair, you change the colour by using different dyes that stain.

E e

each
Each means every one. Each dog has a spot!

eager
If you are eager, you are very keen to do something.

ear
People and animals hear with their ears.

early
Be in good time, be early!

earth
1. We live on a planet called Earth.

2. Another name for soil.

earthquake
When the ground trembles and cracks open.

easel
A stand for a painting or a blackboard.

east
The sun rises in the east. China and Japan are to the east of the map.

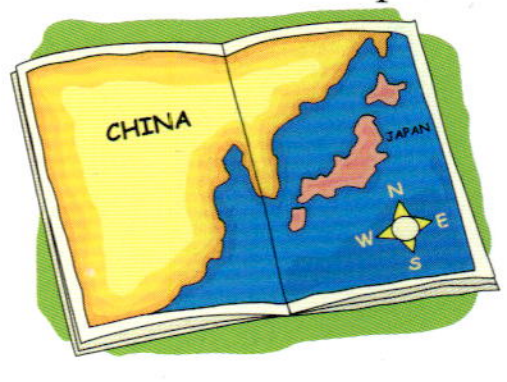

easy
Easy things are simple to understand or do. Never hard or difficult.

eat
When you eat you put food into your mouth, chew it, then swallow.

echo
A sound which bounces back again and again from the walls of mountains or caves.

edge
The end or side of something. Don't fall off the edge!

egg
All birds and a few animals live inside eggs before they hatch.

either
Either means one or the other of two things. You can have either a cake or a carrot.

empty
Empty has nothing in it. My bag was full but now it's empty!

encyclopaedia
A book or several books that contain information on most subjects.

end
The last part or finish of something. This is the end!

engine
The engine makes the power that drives the machine.

enormous
Enormous is very, very big. Do giants have enormous feet?

equal
Things that are equal are the same in size and value.

equator
The imaginary line round the centre of the Earth.

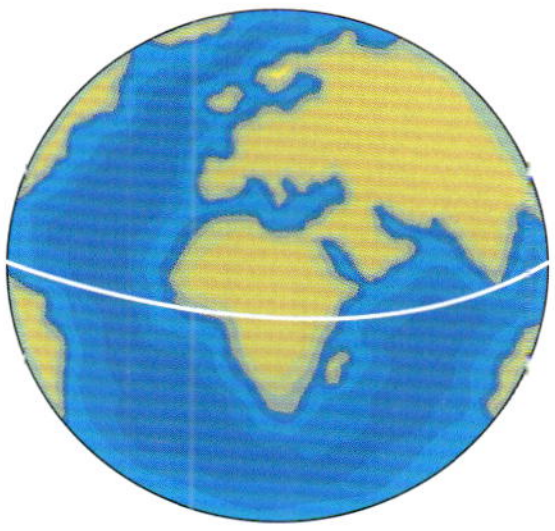

escalator
A moving staircase often in a store or hotel.

escape
To get away, be free. My beetles have escaped!

even
1. An even number can be divided by two.
2. An even surface is flat and smooth.

evening
The end of the day when the sun sets, before night.

electricity
Electricity is power that reaches us along wires. Many machines run on electric power.

emergency
When something very unexpected happens and must be dealt with.

enough
As much as you need and no more. Have you had enough?

enter
When you enter, you go in. You can enter a room. You can also enter a competition.

envelope
A folded paper cover usually for a letter.

ever
Ever means always. I will love you for ever!

every
Every means each one. We get older every minute.

everybody
Everybody means all people. Everybody is born!

everything
Everything means all things. Everything in the room was yellow.

everywhere
Here, there, everywhere; dust gets in all places.

exactly
This piece fits exactly. It is just right.

excellent
Excellent means very, very good. Your exam results are excellent!

excited
To be thrilled with pleasure about something. I am very excited about this trip!

exercise
1. Exercising your body keeps you fit.

2. Doing exercises on the flute helps you to play better.

exit
The way out.

explain
"Can you tell me why you made such a mess?" Then you have to explain.

explode
When something bursts or blows up it explodes with a loud bang.

explore
You can explore a country by going through it and finding new places and things.

extinct
Something that has died out is extinct. The dodo is extinct.

extra
Extra means more than you have. I would like extra gravy on my meat!

extraordinary
Something that is very unusual.

eye
You have two eyes. They are used for seeing. If you have good eyesight, you are able to see well. If you lose your sight and cannot see, you are blind.

eyrie
The nest of an eagle or other bird of prey.

Ff

fable
A fable is a short story with a moral. Aesop wrote many famous fables.

face
At the front of your head under your hair is your face.

fact
A fact is something that can be proved to be true.

fail
To fail is to try but not manage to do something.

fairy
A tiny creature that is believed to be magic. Do you believe in fairies?

fall
Fall means to drop down. An apple has fallen on my head!

false
False means untrue or not real. Is he wearing a false nose?

family
Your family are people related to you.

far
Far is a long way off. The ship sailed far away.

farm
A farm is the land and buildings where crops are grown and animals kept.

farmer
The person who lives and works on the farm.

fast
Fast is very quick. A speedboat is faster than a rowing boat.

fasten
You must fasten your safety belt. If it is closed you will be safe.

father
A father is the male parent of his children.

favourite
Favourite things are the things you like best.

fear
To fear is to feel you are in danger. Are you afraid of the dark?

feather
Feathers cover a bird's body. The large feathers help it to fly and the down helps the bird to keep warm.

feed
To feed is to give someone food. This robin is feeding her young.

feel
To feel something is to handle it and touch it.

fence
If you enclose your garden, you put up a fence as a barrier.

fern
A plant with feathery leaves. Ferns love cool shady places.

few
If you have a few sweets, there are not very many.

field
A piece of land for growing crops or grazing animals.

fierce
Some wild animals are savage and frightening. They are very fierce.

fight
When you fight you argue with someone and often hit them.

figure
A figure is the shape of a number or a person.

fill
To leave no space for any more.

fine
1. A fine day is always warm and sunny.
2. A hair is fine. It is thin lik a thread.

finger
Fingers are at the end of your hands. You have eight fingers and two thumbs.

fire
If something is on fire it is burning. Send for the fire brigade! A fire engine will come as soon as possible . When the blaze is put out the firefighters will return to the fire station.

firework
You must treat fireworks with care because they explode. We all love fireworks on Bonfire Night

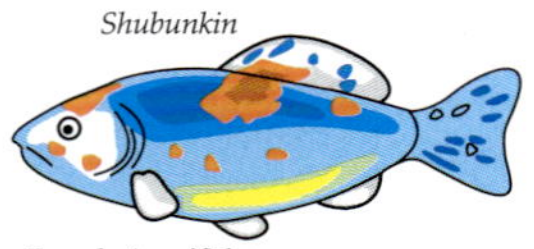

fish
A fish is a swimming anima which lives in the water. They can breathe underwate through their gills.

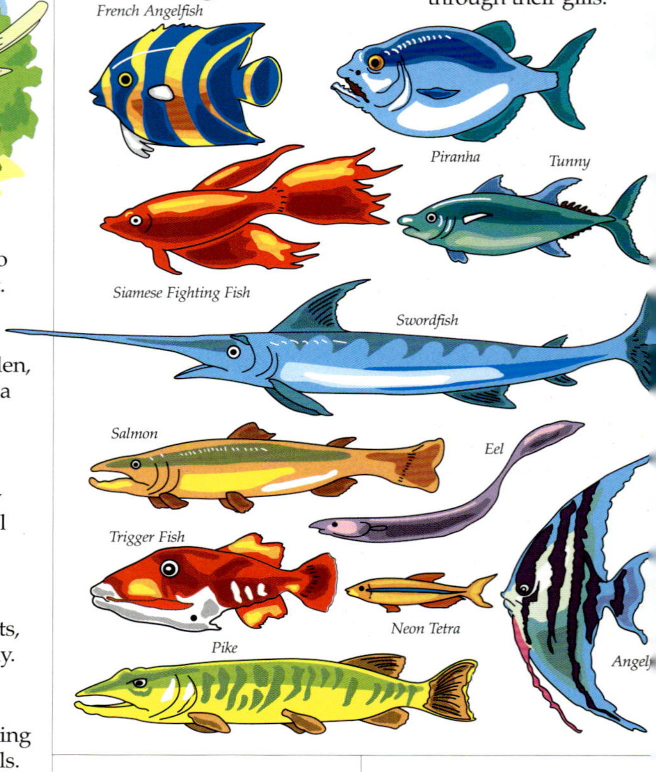

film
1. A film is a moving picture at the cinema or on television.
2. You take photographs on a film inside a camera.

find
To discover something that was lost, or that you didn't know was there.

fit
1. Keep fit, stay healthy.
2. If your shoes do not fit, they are either too big or too small.

fix
1. To mend or repair.
2. To influence something unfairly. That football match was fixed!

flag
A piece of cloth with an emblem on it. Each country has a flag of its own.

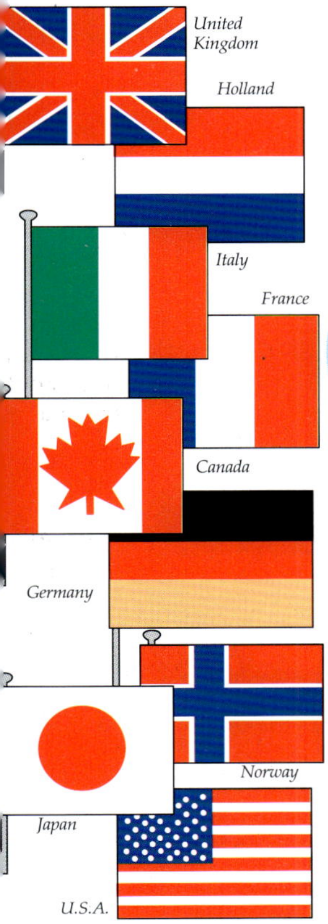

floor
You walk on the floor. It is the lowest part of the room.

flour
Flour is the soft, white powder made from crushed grains of wheat.

fly
1. If you move through the air you fly. Many things fly all by themselves.
2. There is a tiny insect called a fly.

follow
"Follow me," said the fox, "I will lead and you can walk behind."

food
To stay alive we must eat food.

foot
The lowest part of your leg from your ankle to your toe is your foot.

forest
Lots of trees growing together in one big area.

forget
If you don't remember things, you forget them. Have you forgotten the time?

free
1. If a thing is free it costs nothing at all.
2. Prisoners are not free, they cannot come and go as they please.

freeze
When water freezes it gets very cold then turns to ice.

fresh
Fresh means new and clean. Food that is fresh has just been made or picked.

friend
A friend is someone you know very well and like a lot.

fright
What gives you a fright or scares you?

front
Front is the part that faces forward. A man in the front seat of his car is parked in front of the house.

fry
When you fry food you cook it in hot fat or oil.

fun
You laugh when you are having fun.

fur
The hair that covers an animal's body is called fur.

furniture
Houses are full of furniture. We use it every day.

G g

gain
To gain is to increase. It is the opposite of lose.

gale
When there is a gale blowing, the wind is very strong.

gallery
You go to a gallery to see works of art.

game
In any game you play, you must keep to the rules.

garage
A place where cars are kept or repaired.

garden
A garden is a space, usually round a house, for growing flowers and vegetables. You can relax and play in your garden.

gate
A gate is an outside door in a wall, hedge or fence.

geese
A flock of geese is a lot of geese together. One bird on its own is a goose.

flower
Flowers are made up of brightly coloured petals, inside which are the seeds.

fruit
The seeds of a plant grow inside the fruit.

G g

gentle
A gentle person is loving and careful, not rough in any way.

geography
In geography we learn all about the Earth, the animals, the people and the way they all live.

germ
Germs are so tiny you can only see them under a microscope. They can cause disease.

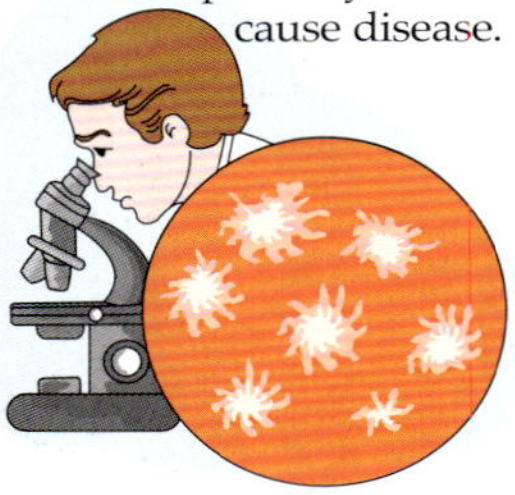

giant
A thing or person that is huge. There are lots of giants in fairy tales.

gift
A gift is a present, something that is given.

girl
When your mother was young she was a girl. A girl grows up to be a woman.

give
If you give a thing away you do not ask for it back.

glad
I am glad you came, means I am very happy that you came.

glass
You can see right through glass. Although it is very hard, it breaks easily.

globe
The globe is shaped like a ball and has a map of the world on its surface.

glove
Gloves cover your hands and keep them warm. They have a separate little cover for each finger.

glue
You can stick things together with glue. It is often very sticky.

go
Go means to leave one place for another. You go your way, I'll go mine.

goal
To score a goal is the purpose of some games.

gold
Gold is a very precious yellow metal.

goggles
They fit tightly to your face and protect your eyes, so you can still see properly.

good
1. He is a good boy, he is well behaved, not naughty.
2. Her work is very good. It is first class!

goodbye
You say goodbye when you are parting from someone.

govern
To govern is to rule and guide people. A government is a group of people who promise to do this.

grab
When you grab something you catch hold of it suddenly. I grabbed a bun before mother grabbed me!

grandfather
My father's father and my mother's father are my grandfathers.

grandmother
My father's mother and my mother's mother are my grandmothers.

grass
Grass is green with thin sword-shaped leaves.

great
1. Abraham Lincoln was a great man. He was an important man. He became President of the United States of America.

2. A great shadow fell across the path. It was a very big shadow.

greedy
A greedy person always wants more for himself.

greenhouse
A building made of glass where plants are grown.

grin
A great big smile!

ground
Everyone walks on the ground. It is the Earth's surface.

grow
To grow is to get bigger. My how you've grown!

guard
The soldiers are on guard looking after the Queen and keeping her safe.

guardian
Someone who looks after, defends, or is responsible for someone or something.

guess
To say or think something you don't really know.

guide
To guide is to show the way. Guide-dogs lead blind people.

gun
A dangerous weapon that fires bullets. Cowboys carry guns.

gymnasium
A large room where people keep fit on special apparatus.

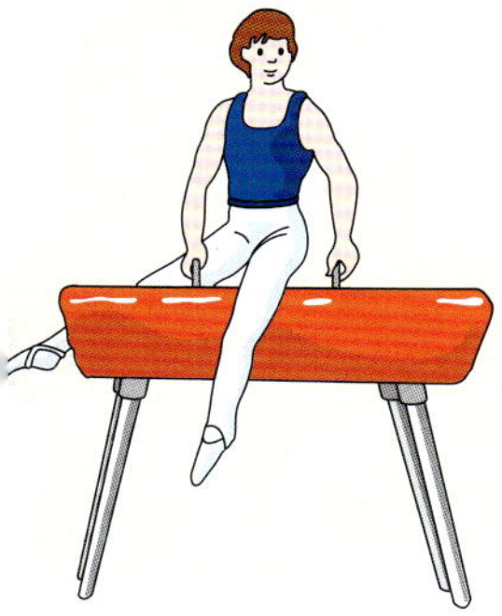

hair
Hair grows on the bodies of animals and humans. Some people are more hairy than others.

half
If you cut something in half you get two pieces of equal size. Each one is called a half.

Hallowe'en
The thirty-first of October is Hallowe'en, the night that witches fly about!

halt
When you are told to halt, you must stop moving at once!

hamburger
A round, flat cake of minced beef, often served in a bread bun.

handle
A hammer has a handle. Be careful how you handle it!

handwriting
The way you write with a pen or pencil.

happen
When something happens, it takes place. What happened to you?

happy
Full of joy and very pleased about things.

hard
1. Hard is difficult, not easy to do.
2. Hard also means solid and firm. Hard as iron!

harm
To do harm is to hurt or damage a person or thing.

harvest
To gather in all the crops when they are ready.

hat
You wear a hat to cover and protect your head.

hate
To hate is to really dislike a thing. I hate washing dishes!

have
If you have a thing, you own it. I have long hair now, when I was a baby I had none at all.

head
1. The top part of a person's or animal's body.
2. It can also mean the chief or most important thing or person.

health
Your health is how your body feels. Healthy is well, unhealthy is ill.

hear
You hear sounds through your ears when you listen.

heart
Your heart is like a pump that sends the blood round your body.

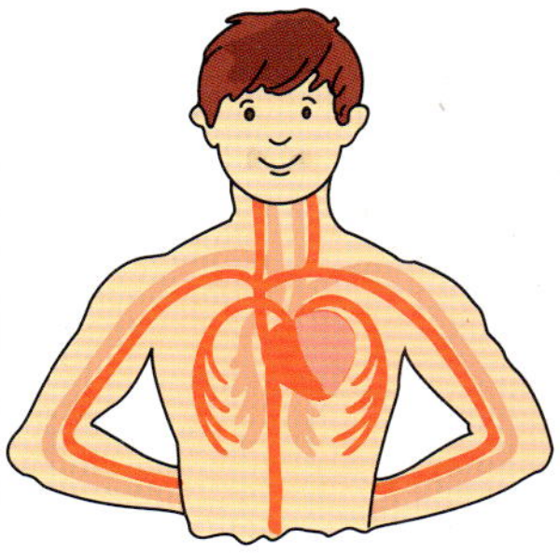

heat
Hot things give off heat.

heavy
Something heavy weighs a lot.

heel
The back of your foot or the back of your shoe is a heel.

height
Measure your height from the ground to the top of your head.

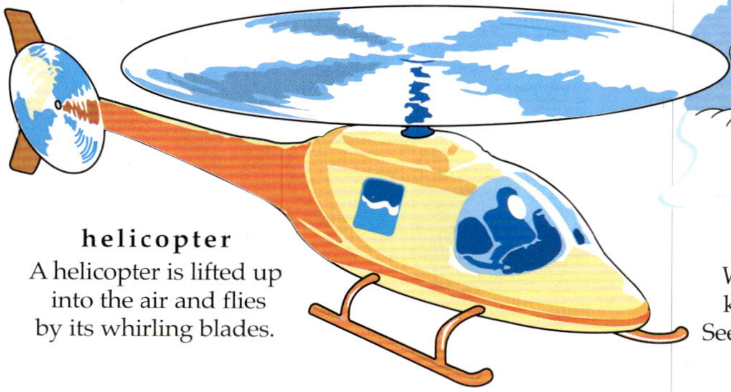

helicopter
A helicopter is lifted up into the air and flies by its whirling blades.

hello
Hello is a greeting. When you answer the telephone you say hello!

helmet
A helmet is a hard hat which protects the head.

help
To help is to make things easier for another person. I will help you paint the fence!

herbs
Each herb has a different smell and flavour. These plants are used for medicine and food.

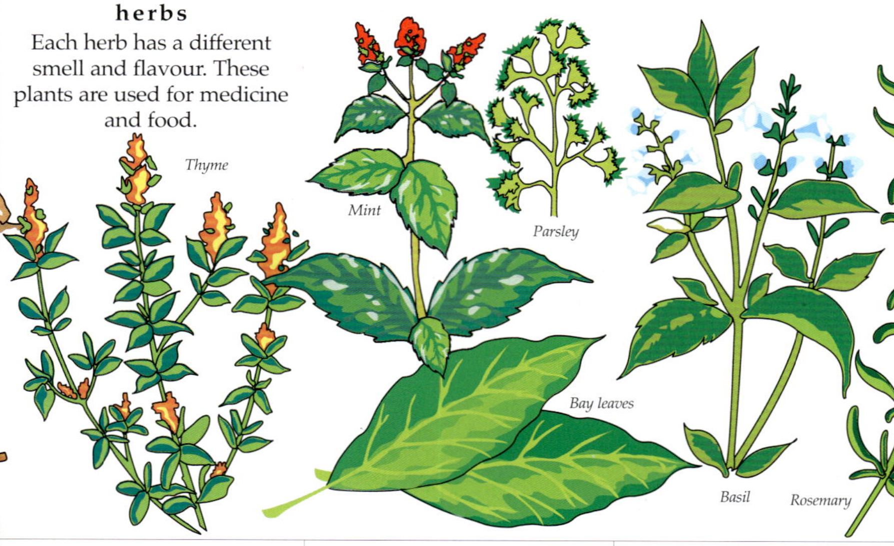

here
Here is the place you are at this moment. I live here!

hero
A hero is a very brave man or boy.

heroine
A heroine is a very brave woman or girl.

hesitate
To be reluctant to do something or to hold back. She hesitated before climbing up the ladder.

hexagon
A six-sided shape.

hibernate
When the weather turns cold some animals hibernate and go to sleep for the winter.

hide
Will you hide him and keep him out of sight? See that he is well hidden!

high
Mountains are very high. They are a long way from the ground.

hill
A hill is a small mountain with gently sloping sides.

hint
To suggest, without saying something clearly. Joe's friend hinted that he would like to stay for tea.

hire
1. To pay to use something for a given period of time.
2. To employ someone to do some work.

his
His means belonging to a man. Is that jacket really his?

history
History is the story of the past. Learning history is often hard!

hit
Hit is to strike out or knock something or someone.

hold
This tin holds biscuits. Hold out your hand and you can have one!

hole
A hole is an opening. It can go right through a thing, or it can form a hollow.

hollow
A hollow has nothing but empty space inside. The conjuror showed us a hollow tube.

home
Home is where you live.

homework
Work brought from school to be done at home.

honest
To be honest is to be truthful.

hook
A bent piece of metal for catching hold of things.

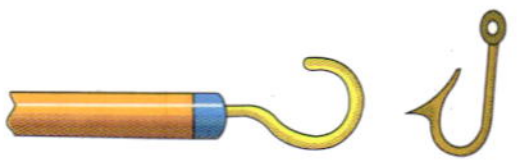

hop
To bob up and down on one foot. Who is this hopping along?

hope
I hope my wish will come true! You really want your wish to happen.

horizon
The horizon is the place where the ground and the sky seem to meet.

horn

1. The hard part that sticks out of an animal's head.

Rhino

Antelope

Deer

2. Have you a horn on your bicycle?

hospital

If you have had an accident or you are ill you go to hospital to be taken care of.

hot

Do not touch hot things. They give off heat and could burn you.

hotel

When you are away from home, you can pay for a room and a meal in a hotel.

hour

Sixty minutes in one hour, twenty-four hours in a day.

hovercraft

A hovercraft carries passengers just above the sea or land on a cushion of air.

how

This is an asking word; how was that done?

human

People, because they think and speak, are human. Animals are not.

hungry

I am hungry. I need some food because I lost my lunch!

hurricane

A violent storm with strong winds that can cause a lot of damage.

hurry

To be quick or rush. Hurry up, or we will miss the bus!

hurt

Someone who is hurt is in pain. I bet that hurts!

hutch

A home for a pet rabbit.

hydrogen

A colourless gas, which combines with oxygen to make water.

hymn

A song of praise to God.

hypnosis

A trance-like state in which the person is open to suggestion.

I i

ice

Ice is frozen water. It is solid, cold and hard.

iceberg

An iceberg is a mountain of ice floating in the sea.

ice-cream

Ice-cream is cream and sugar frozen. If you lick it, it melts in your mouth.

icicle

A spike of ice hanging down where water has dripped and frozen into a point.

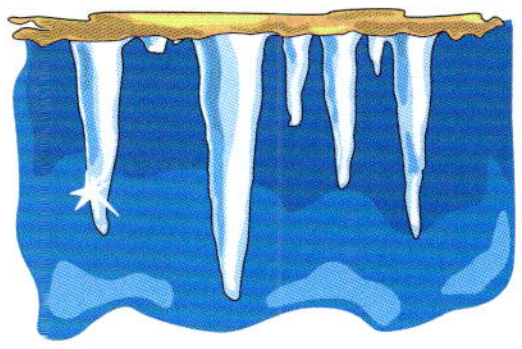

idea

When Sally has a clever idea, she has a clever thought in her mind.

ill

My brother feels unwell today. I'm sure he is ill.

immediately

"Take that make-up off immediately!" She means at once.

impossible

It is impossible to count all the grains of sand. It can't be done.

indoors

Table tennis is an indoor game, it is played inside.

infant

A very young child is an infant. It can be a boy or a girl.

injure

The skier hit a pine tree and was injured. He was hurt badly.

ink

Your pen is full of a coloured liquid called ink.

insect

There are many different kinds of insects, all have six legs.

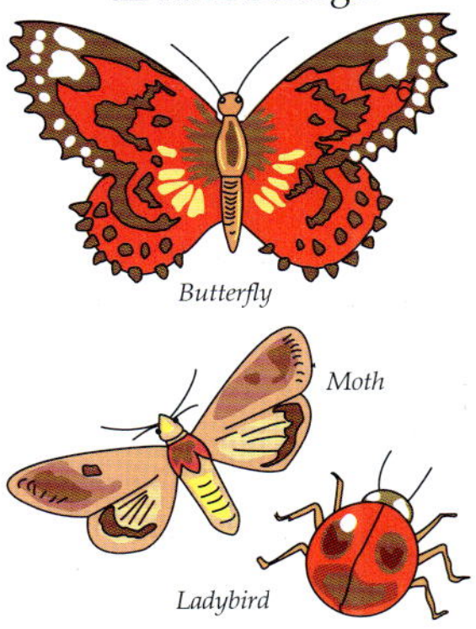

Butterfly

Moth

Ladybird

inside
You can be inside a room and inside the cupboard. You are not outside, you are within.

instant
Quick as a flash! In an instant, the wizard turned the frog into a prince.

introduce
Baby Bear introduced the little girl to his Mummy and Daddy. "This is Goldilocks!" he said.

inventor
An inventor thinks of something useful that no one has ever thought of before.

invisible
Something invisible cannot be seen.

invite
To invite is to ask someone to do something. Here is an invitation to my party.

iron
1. A hard metal that is used to make steel.
2. I will iron your jeans with my new iron!

island
An island is land surrounded by water. Fiji is a small island, Australia is a huge one.

instrument
Music is played on an instrument. Here are some of them.

jacket
A jacket is a short coat. It can also mean a cover or an outer casing.

jail
When you are sent to prison you are put in jail.

jam
1. Jam is made by boiling sugar and fruit together.

2. When things are squeezed tightly together they are jammed. These cars are in a traffic jam.

jar
A jar is a container with a wide opening at the top. Jars often hold food.

jaw
The base of your mouth to which your teeth are fixed.

jealous
I am jealous because she won the cup. I want it, although it belongs to her!

jeans
Trousers made from a thick, cotton cloth called denim.

jelly
Jelly is made from fruit juice and gelatine. When set, it is clear and wobbly.

jellyfish
A jellyfish drifts in the sea. Its body is like a jelly and it can sting you!

jet
1. A fast stream of liquid or gas.
2. A hard black stone.

3. A very fast aircraft driven by a jet engine, not propellers. The engine makes hot gases which escape backwards and thrust the plane forwards.

jewel
A jewel is a precious stone.

jewellery
An ornament made of gold and silver and jewels.

jigsaw
A picture cut up into pieces for you to fit together again.

job
This man is a milkman. It is his job to deliver the milk.

jog
When horses jog they trot slowly. People jog to keep fit.

join
1. When you join two things, you fasten them together.

2. When you join a club you become a member. Join the Brownies!

joke
A joke is a short story that makes you laugh. Have you heard this joke?

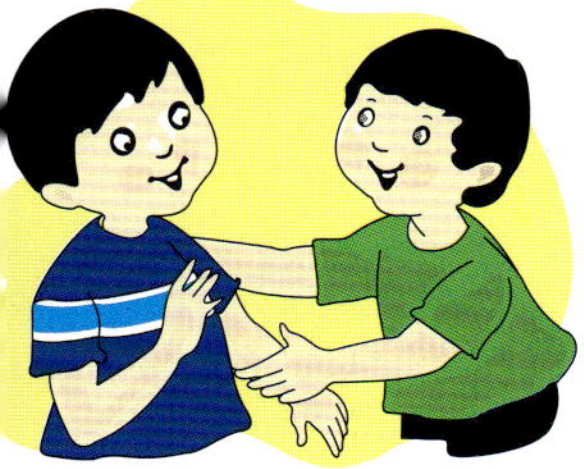

jolly
When we hear lots of jokes we feel jolly.

journey
When you go on a journey you travel to a place. It can be a short or long trip.

joy
When you jump for joy, you are delighted.

judge
A person who decides what is right and what is wrong in a dispute.

jug
A jug holds liquids and is very easy to pour.

juggernaut
A huge lorry.

juggler
Jugglers entertain you by balancing objects and keeping them in the air at the same time.

juice
The liquid squeezed from fruit and vegetables.

jumbo
Anything very large, often used to refer to an elephant.

jump
Spring into the air with both feet off the ground.

junction
The place where two or more routes meet.

jungle
A jungle is a tropical forest, it is dense and overgrown.

jury
The group of people who decide whether or not someone is guilty at a trial. A jury can also be the judges of a competition.

kilogramme
The weight of something is measured in kilogrammes.

K k

keen
If you are keen, you are very willing to do things.

keep
To keep is to hold onto something. A miser keeps all his money to himself.

ketchup
A thick, tasty sauce for food.

kettle
You boil water in a kettle. It has a spout for pouring out the water.

key
A key fits into a keyhole. You must turn it to unlock the door.

kick
When you kick you strike out with your foot. Kick the ball, not your brother

kill
Kill is to make something or someone die.

kind
1. Kind means caring towards others.
2. What kind of fruit would you like? This means what sort.

king
A king rules his country or kingdom.

kitchen
You prepare and cook food in the kitchen. You wash-up there too!

kite
A kite is made up of paper or cloth on a wooden frame. It flies high in the sky lifted by the wind.

kitten
A young cat. Kittens always love to play.

knife
A cutting implement with a sharp edge, used for eating or as a weapon.

knee
This is the joint that makes your leg bend, especially when you kneel.

knight
Long ago knights wore armour and fought on horseback.

knit
When you knit you make a garment by weaving loops of wool together on needles.

knob
A round lump on the end or surface of something. When you open a door you turn the knob.

knock
Knock at the door, but not too hard, or you will knock it down!

knot
When you tie a knot you join two pieces of string together.

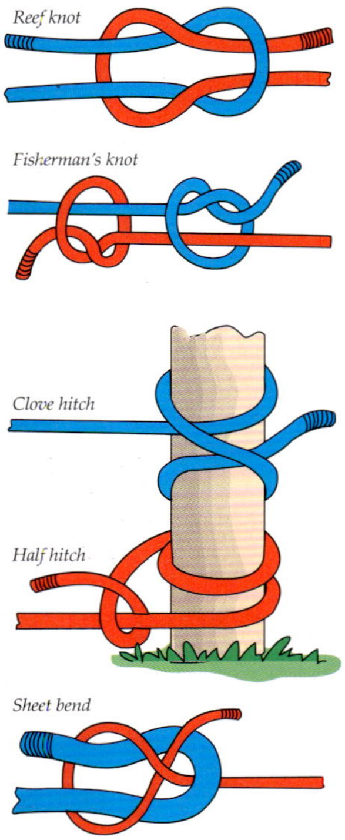

know
Do you understand how to tie knots? Do you know how to do them? I knew you did!

L l

label
A label tells you about a thing or what is inside.

ladder
You climb up the rungs of a ladder to reach high places. Window cleaners always carry their ladders around.

lake
A large stretch of water with land all around.

lamp
There are many different kinds of lamps and they all give us light.

land
1. Land is the surface of the Earth that is not sea.
2. Concorde is about to land at the airport.

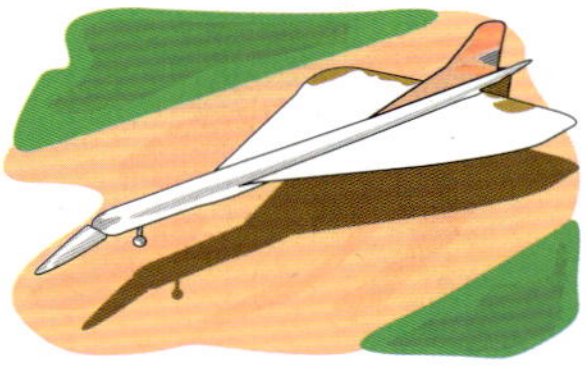

lane
A narrow road in the country. A narrow street in the town.

language
Words used by people to write and speak. There are many different languages.

large
Large is big, not little.

lasso
A cowboy uses a lasso for roping cattle. It is a long rope with a sliding loop.

last
1. Last means after all the others.
2. How long will this noise last? How long will it go on?

late
If you are late for school you arrive later than you should.

laugh
When people see something funny they laugh. Ha! Ha!

launch
When you launch a rocket into space or a ship into the sea, you start it moving.

lawn
An area of grass in a garden. It is cut by a lawnmower to keep it short.

lay
1. Birds lay eggs. They produce them.
2. When we lay something down, we put it down carefully.

lazy
If you are lazy, you don't want to do any work.

lead
1. To lead is to show the way.
2. A dog has a lead. It is a strap that fits onto his collar.

learn
You learn if you find out facts or get to know how to do things.

leave
When baby birds leave the nest they go away. Leave them alone, they will be back next year!

left
Left is opposite to right.

leg
Tables, chairs and people are supported by legs.

legend
Some say Robin Hood was a legend. Do you believe he was real or just a story?

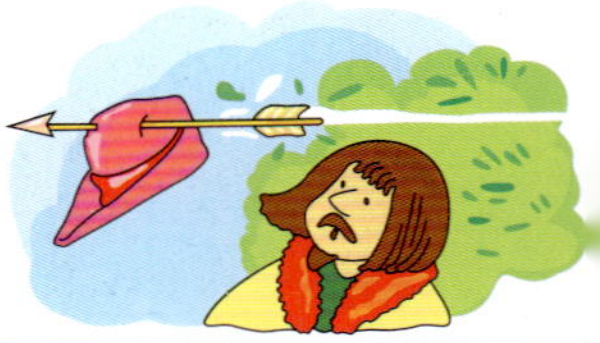

leaf
Here are some different leaf shapes. Leaves cover trees and plants.

lemonade
A drink made from lemons, water and sugar. It can be very fizzy.

lend
To lend is to let a person borrow something for a little while.

length
The distance from one end to the other.

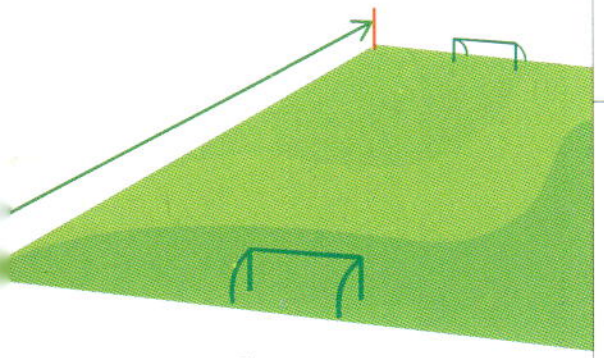

less
Less is not as much. I get less pocket money than Jim!

lesson
A certain length of time in which you learn.

letter
1. You can write a message to someone in a letter.
2. Twenty-six letters make up the alphabet.

library
A place where collections of books are kept. Borrow a book from your library!

lichen
Small, flowerless plants that grow on plants and trees.

lid
A lid is a cover that closes a container.

lie
1. When you don't tell the truth, you lie.
2. When you lie down, you remain flat.

life
Everything alive has life. Life is being alive.

lifeboat
A special boat full of brave men who try to save people from drowning in the sea.

lift
To raise something up higher. Lift me up!

light
1. Things that are not heavy are light.
2. Light comes from the Sun and at night we must use lamps.

lighthouse
You will find a lighthouse near dangerous coasts. The winking light on top of the tower warns sailors of danger.

lightning
It flashes in the sky during a thunderstorm.

like
1. If you like a person, you are fond of them.
2. Like can mean almost the same.

line
Draw a line!

It can be straight or it can be curved.

lipstick
Make-up for your lips. Have I got too much lipstick on?

liquid
You can pour a liquid. It flows and is always wet.

listen
If you want to hear a sound, you must listen.

litre
A litre is a measurement used to measure liquids.

1 litre is about 1 1/4 pints

little
Little means very small.

live
I live in a house, my fish lives in a bowl. I can't live in the water, he can't live out of it!

lobster
A shellfish with a tough shell and two very strong pincers.

lock
A lock fastens a door, a chest or a drawer. You must have the right key to unlock it.

long
How long is the pencil? How far is it from one end to the other?

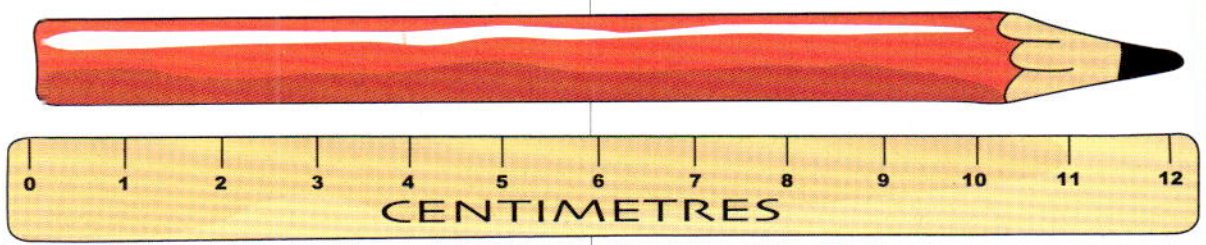

look
Look up, look down, look all around! You are using your eyes to see.

loose
If you have a loose tooth, it is not fixed. It wobbles!

lorry
A lorry is a truck that moves goods from place to place by road.

lose
When you lose something, although you search, you can't find it.

lot
What a lot of lettuces. I've never seen so many!

loud
You can hear a loud noise very easily.

love
To love someone is to like them as much as you can. I love my little baby sister so much. I want to cuddle her all the time!

luggage
When you go on holiday you take bags and cases full of clothes and other items that you will need. Lots of luggage!

lull
To soothe or calm. I will lull my baby to sleep with a gentle lullaby.

lumberjack
A man who cuts down trees ready for the mill.

lunch
A midday meal. It might be a quick snack or a great big bite!

M m

machine
Machines help us do our work easier and quicker. Here are a few that help us.

Lawn tractor

Hand mixer

Vacuum cleaner

Garden tiller

magic
No one can explain magic. Strange things happen when magic spells are cast!

magnet
Magnets are made of iron and steel. They attract or pull metal objects towards them.

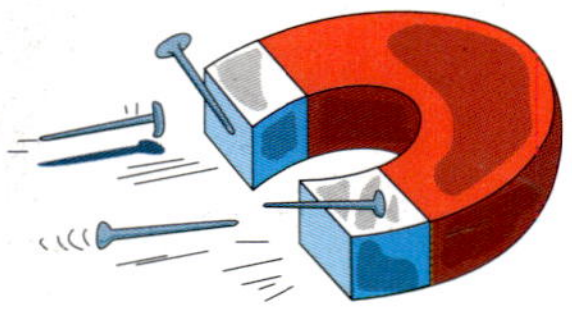

magnify
Magnify is to make things bigger. Look under this magnifying glass.

make
If you make something you put it together. You make the dinner today!

male
Male is the opposite of female. Men and boys are male.

man
When a boy grows up he becomes a man.

many
Many means a lot. A Dalmatian has many spots.

map
A map is a plan of a continent, a country or just a small area.

march
To march is to walk in step like soldiers.

margarine
This food is made from a blend of vegetable oils. You can spread it on bread or cook with it.

market
Lots of things are bought and sold from stalls in the market. Some markets are held out of doors.

marry
When a man and woman become husband and wife they marry.

mask
A mask covers your face. It can make you look very different.

match
1. You can light a match.
2. You can play in a match.
3. You can match things up.

meadow
A grass field full of wild flowers and plants.

meal
Breakfast, lunch, tea and supper are meals.

measure
When we measure something, we find out the size of it or how much there is.

mechanic
A person who looks after engines.

medicine
If you are ill, medicine will help you get well.

meet
I am going to meet my pen friend! We are going to get together.

melt
The sun came out and my snowman turned to water. He melted!

mend
To mend is to repair something so it will be useful again.

mermaid
A legendary sea creature with a woman's body and a fish's tail for legs.

mess
If your room is a mess, it is very untidy.

message
When you send a message, you send words to another person.

metal
Iron, steel, aluminium, copper and tin are all metals.

method
A method is a well thought out way to do something.

metre
A metre is a measurement of length or height.

microphone
It picks up sounds and makes them louder. Pick up the mike!

microscope
Tiny objects appear much bigger under a microscope.

midday
Midday is twelve noon.

middle
The middle is a point in the centre, the same distance from either end.

midnight
Twelve o'clock at night, before a new day begins.

milk
We drink milk from cows and sometimes goats.

million
A thousand thousand.

miner
A man who works down a mine.

minus
1. Uncle is minus his glasses. He can't see without them.
2. Minus also means to subtract.

10 - 6 = 4

minute
Sixty seconds in a minute. Sixty minutes in one hour.

mirror
Look in the mirror! What do you see reflected in the glass?

miserable
When my parrot escaped, I felt very miserable.

miss
1. I miss my parrot so much. I wish he would come back!
2. I love to play in goal but I often miss the ball!

mist
Mist is like a fine rain or a light fog.

mistake
To make a mistake is to make an error.

2 + 2 = ~~5~~ 4

mix
If you put different things together you mix them.

money
We use money when we buy things. We pay in coins and notes.

monster
A monster is a huge, horrible, frightening thing.

month
There are twelve months in a year.

JANUARY · FEBRUARY · MARCH
APRIL · MAY · JUNE · JULY
AUGUST · SEPTEMBER · OCTOBER
NOVEMBER · DECEMBER

moon
The Moon spins round the Earth. The Sun's light catches the Moon and makes it shine.

moonlight
When the Moon is full it shines with a silvery light called moonlight.

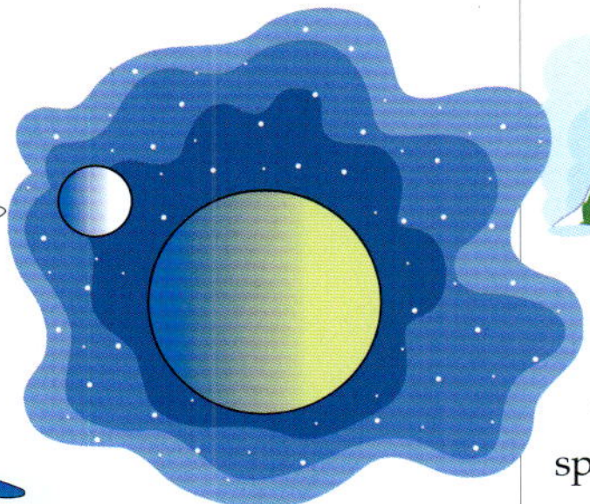

more
Mary has more apples than Ken. She has a greater amount.

morning
The morning comes after the night and goes on until midday.

most
Sara has the most flowers. She has the greater amount.

moth
Moths are not as colourful as butterflies. They fly at night.

Tiger

Hawk

Emperor

mother
A mother is a woman who has had a child or children.

mug
You get more in a mug than a cup. What is your favourite drink – maybe a nice mug of hot chocolate?

mule
A cross between a horse and an ass.

multiply
You make something several times bigger if you multiply.

6 × 4 = 24

muscle
Muscles are parts of the body that produce movement, they can only pull not push. We need two sets of muscles for each joint or limb, one to bend and one to straighten.

museum
A place where you can look at collections of interesting or historical things.

music
Different sounds made by instruments or a person's voice are music.

mystery
A mystery is something strange or puzzling that you cannot explain.

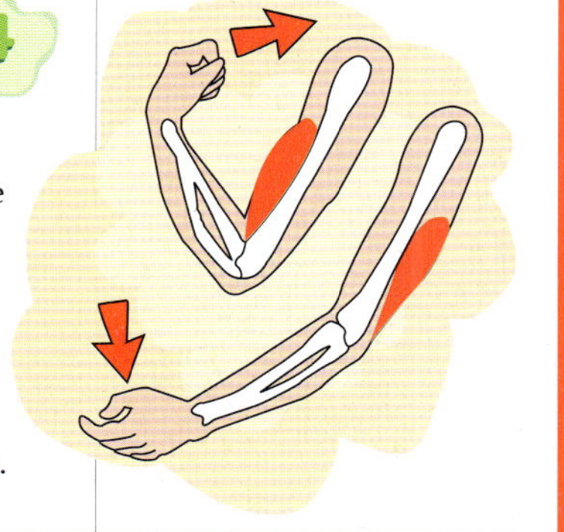

motorway
A modern fast road with three lanes in each direction.

mountain
A gigantic hill with steep rocky sides. Some mountain peaks are covered in snow.

mouth
You use your mouth to speak and eat. Smile please!

move
Nothing stands still, even the Earth is moving all the time.

mud
Wet, sticky, soft earth is mud. Wipe your muddy boots!

N n

nail
1. A thin piece of metal with a sharp point. You hammer it through two pieces of wood to join them together.

2. Nails are the hard parts on the tips of your fingers and toes.

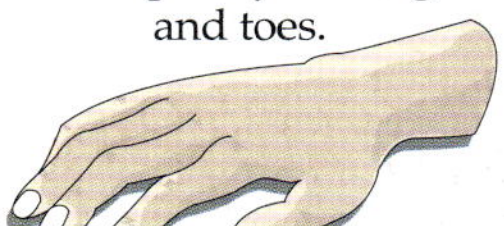

name
Each person and every thing has a name. That is what they are called.

narrow
This opening is too narrow to squeeze through. It isn't wide enough!

nib
A nib is a pen point.

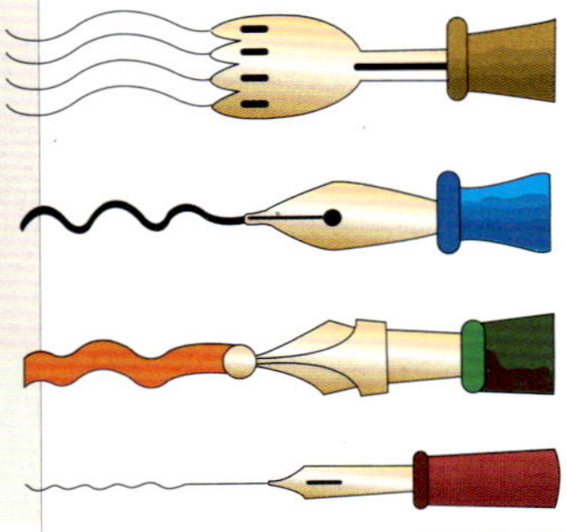

north
North is opposite to south. The Arctic Circle and the North Pole are the coldest northern parts of the world.

nasty
How unpleasant. What a nasty black eye!

natural
Made by nature and not by man.

nature
The world around us, not changed by man in any way.

naughty
To behave badly in a mischievous way.

navy
The whole of a country's ships of war and all the sailors.

need
When you need a thing it is necessary to have it. This gentleman needs a new suit!

needle
A thin pointed piece of metal with a slit at one end. Poke a thread through the slit and you can begin to sew.

nest
Most birds and a few animals make a nest for their young.

near
Near is close. I was so near to the shark I could have touched it!

nearly
He nearly fell in the river means he almost did.

nectar
Honey of flowers that bees collect.

neat
When you are neat you are tidy and put everything in the proper place.

neighbour
Someone who lives near by.

nervous
I am frightened of the shadows in my room. They make me very nervous.

net
A net is for catching things without doing any damage.

never
Never is at no time, not ever. You will never be able to lift that!

nettle
A plant that stings if you touch it.

new
Something that has never been worn or has just been made. New is fresh, not old.

newspaper
Printed sheets of paper to read. They tell you the news every day.

next
You are next in line, so you can sit next to the driver. Next to means near, next means coming after.

nibble
Take little bites of something. Hamsters nibble their food.

nice
Nice means pleasant or kind. It can also mean dainty or accurate.

night
When the sun has set, it grows dark and night falls.

nobody
If a room is empty, there is nobody there!

noise
A sound of any kind. Susan was making too much noise in class, so the teacher told her off.

none
Paul had six bricks, Peter had none, not even one.

nonsense
Something silly.

noon
Noon is twelve o'clock midday.

nose
You breathe and smell through your nose.

not
You are not to throw that! Not is another way of saying no.

note
1. Mum wrote Dad a note about his dinner.

2. When you play a tune, you hear and play lots notes.

nothing
Nothing on your plate means not one thing.

notice
1. A notice is a written sign for all to read.

2. Have you noticed Tom's arm? Have you seen it?

nought
Nought is the name of the figure 0.

noun
A noun is the name of anything from apple to zebra.

now
I am going for a walk now. Now means at this very moment.

nowhere
My hat is nowhere in sight. I can't see it anywhere.

nuisance
Something that is annoying. That bonfire is a nuisance.

number
A symbol or word that says how many.

nurse
A person trained to look after the sick.

nursery
A place where little children play and are looked after.

O o

oak
The oak is the traditional tree of England. This great tree grows from a tiny acorn.

oar
You row a boat with oars.

oasis
A fertile place in the desert with water and trees.

obey
The Genie of the Lamp obeyed Aladdin. He did as Aladdin told him.

occupation
What is this man's occupation? What job does he do?

ocean
An ocean is bigger than a sea.

o'clock
When we tell the time by the clock we say four o'clock.

octopus
A sea creature with eight arms or tentacles.

odd
1. An odd number cannot be divided by two like an even number.
2. Something strange or out of the ordinary. Sophie didn't wave to me today. That's odd.

off
Switch off the television! Jump off the chair! Off means not on.

offer
If you say you will do something, you offer to help. Mother offered Tom a lift.

office
People work in an office. It is their place of business.

officer
Someone who is in command and gives orders to people in the navy, army, airforce, the police or the fire service.

often
My dog often digs in the garden. He does it again and again.

ogre
A fairy-tale monster or man-eating giant.

oil
1. Oil is a greasy, black liquid that is found underground or under the sea bed.

Drilling for oil at sea

2. We use oil made from seeds and plants for cooking.

ointment
Put some ointment on your knees, they look sore!

old
An old person has lived a long time. An old thing has been used a lot and is no longer new.

only
James was the only one to win a rosette. No one else did, he was the only one.

open
Open means not shut. Alice went through the open door and opened her eyes wide.

opera
A musical play with singers instead of actors.

nut
A nut has a hard shell with a kernel or seed inside.

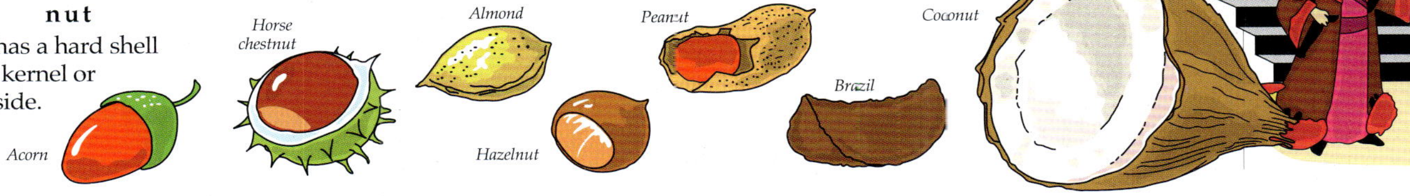

orchard
Fruit trees grow in an orchard.

orchestra
Many musicians playing together form an orchestra. Their instruments are in four different groups.

ordinary
Something ordinary has nothing special about it. What an ordinary house!

ornament
Ornaments are a decoration. We get pleasure from seeing them.

other
Here are two kittens, one is ginger, the other grey. One is different to the other.

our
Our ball has been stolen. It belonged to us.

out
We are going out to play. The sun is shining outside and we don't want to stay in.

outline
Draw an outline of your pet.

oval
Anything oval is shaped like an egg.

oven
You can roast and bake food in an oven.

over
1. The hen flew over the gate.
2. I am sad my holiday is over, or at an end.

overhead
The swans flew overhead. They passed above our heads.

overwhelm
To overwhelm is to crush or submerge. The noise in the football stadium was so overwhelming that Sandy left. It was just too much.

owe
If you owe money to someone then you have borrowed it and will have to pay it back.

owl
A bird of prey that flies at night.

own
If you own something it belongs to you. I own a puppy called Goldie.

ox
A bull or cow.

oxygen
Oxygen is one of the gases in air that all living things must have to live.

Pp

pack
Father wants me to pack his shorts, but the case is packed to the brim. It is full up.

paddle
1. Oh dear! My paddle is floating away.
2. I took my baby sister for a paddle in the shallow water.

page
A page is one side of a piece of paper in a book, magazine or newspaper.

pain
When you feel a pain it hurts. Your body is telling your brain something is wrong.

paint
If you paint a picture or a house, you are putting colour on with a brush.

pair
A pair is two of the same thing. They go together.

palm
1. Dates and coconuts grow on palm trees. People use their leaves to thatch huts and make mats.

2. Hold out your hand, the inside or front is your palm.

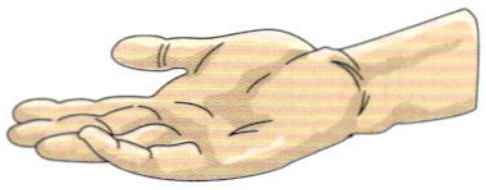

Can you toss a pancake? A batter made of eggs, flour and milk is poured into a frying-pan and cooked into a pancake.

paper
Paper is made from pulped up wood, which is pressed and rolled into sheets.

parachute
When you jump out of a plane your parachute opens like an umbrella, and you float safely downwards.

parcel
Something wrapped in paper and fastened with string or tape.

parents
Mothers and fathers are parents.

park
1. An open space with grass and trees that everyone can use.
2. Have I parked my car in the wrong place?

party
A party is a group of people. When people celebrate they love a party!

pass
1. That motorbike is going to pass us.
2. I have lost my bus pass.
3. The cowboy rode through the mountain pass.
4. My auntie has passed her driving test at last.
5. Pass the ketchup please!

passenger
A person who travels in a plane, boat, train or motor vehicle.

passport
You need your passport to travel from one country to another.

past
Something that happened in the past, usually means it happened long ago.

pastry
When you rub fat into flour and roll it out with a rolling pin, you have made pastry.

pat
If you pat your dog you tap him gently to show you are pleased with him.

pattern
1. Do you like to draw or paint a pattern?
2. A dress pattern has shapes that fit together on material. Cut out and sewn together, they make a dress.

pay
When you buy something, you must pay for it with money.

peace
Peace means no fighting or war. It can also mean quiet and calm. How peaceful!

peanut
Peanuts grow underground. Have you tasted roasted peanuts and peanut butter?

pearl
If you are lucky you may find a pearl in an oyster. You need lots of pearls to make a necklace.

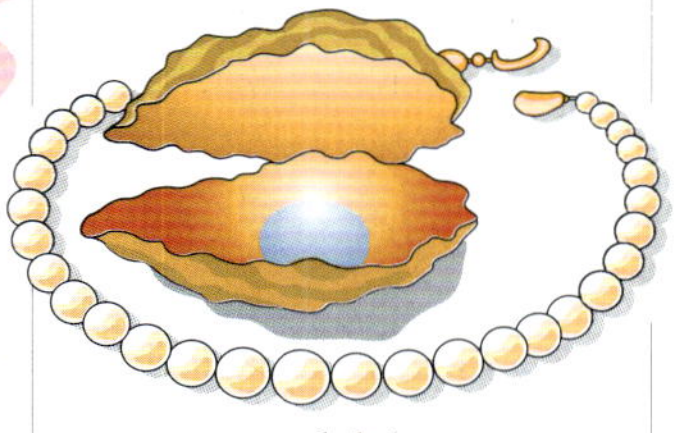

pebble
Little smooth stones found on beaches or river-beds.

pedal
When you pedal your bicycle with your feet on the pedals, you make the wheels move.

peel
The peel is the skin of fruit and vegetables. This apple has been peeled.

paw
Animals have paws. Who made these paw marks?

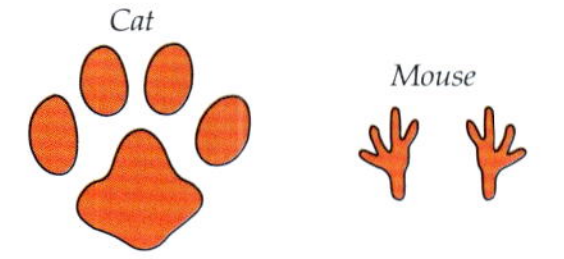

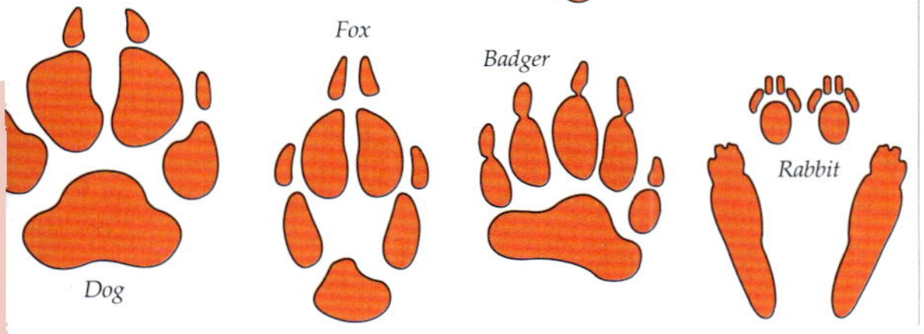

pen
You use a pen for writing with ink.

pencil
A pencil is a wooden stick with a thin lead through the middle.

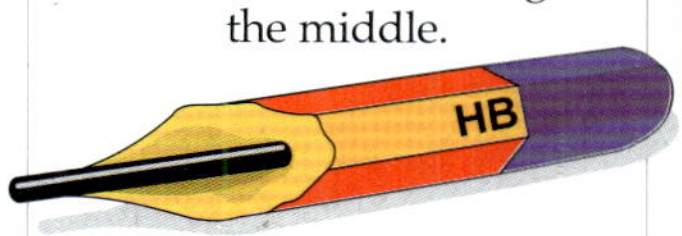

penguin
A flightless bird that lives in arctic conditions.

peninsula
A bit of land that is almost surrounded by water.

penknife
A knife small enough to keep in your pocket. It has blades that fit into the handle.

people
Men, women and children are all people.

perfect
When a thing is perfect it has no faults at all. Your sewing is perfect!

perform
If you perform something, you carry it out or do it. What a performance!

perfume
A sweet smelling scent from flowers or in a bottle.

person
Every single man, woman and child is a person. Animals are not.

pet
An animal kept at home in your house or garden.

phobia
A fear of something. Many people have a phobia of spiders.

photograph
A picture taken with a camera. Do you like having your photo taken?

piano
When you play the piano and your fingers press the keys, lots of tiny hammers hit wires and make the different notes.

pick
1. If you pick flowers you collect or gather them up.

2. Pick a card! You can choose any one.

picnic
A packed meal eaten out of doors.

picture
A picture is a drawing or a painting. It can also be a photograph.

pie
Something good to eat inside a pastry crust.

piece
If you take a piece of pie, you take part of it.

pile
Things heaped up on top of each other are in a pile.

pill
A pill is medicine made into a little ball or easy-to-swallow shape.

pillar
Posts that hold up porches, arches and buildings.

pillow
A soft cushion on a bed.

pilot
A pilot steers an aeroplane.

pin
Shaped like a small needle with a tiny round head at one end.

pipe
1. Does your grandad smoke a pipe?

2. Pipes can carry liquid or gas. They are hollow tubes.

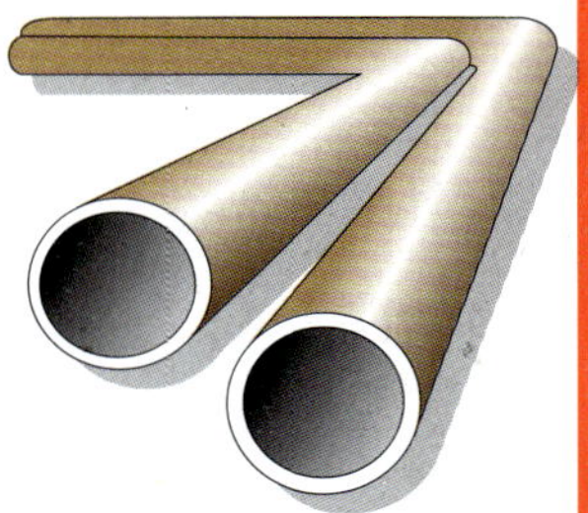

place
This is my place at the table! It is your special spot where you are.

plait
Strands of hair or lengths of material woven into a pattern.

plan
1. A plan is a drawing of an object or a building from above.
2. Those naughty boys have a plan. Have you any idea what it is?

platform
1. A raised floor like a small stage.
2. I sat on the platform waiting for the train.

play
1. A play is a story which is acted out in front of an audience.

2. When you play, forget work and have fun!
3. You play a musical instrument. Harry can play the xylophone very well.

plough
A tractor or horse pulls a plough as it cuts and turns the soil.

plug
A thing that fits into a hole.

plunge
Sam plunged into the water.

polite
If you have good manners and behave well, people will say you are polite.

planet
There are nine major planets that spin round the Sun. The Earth is one.

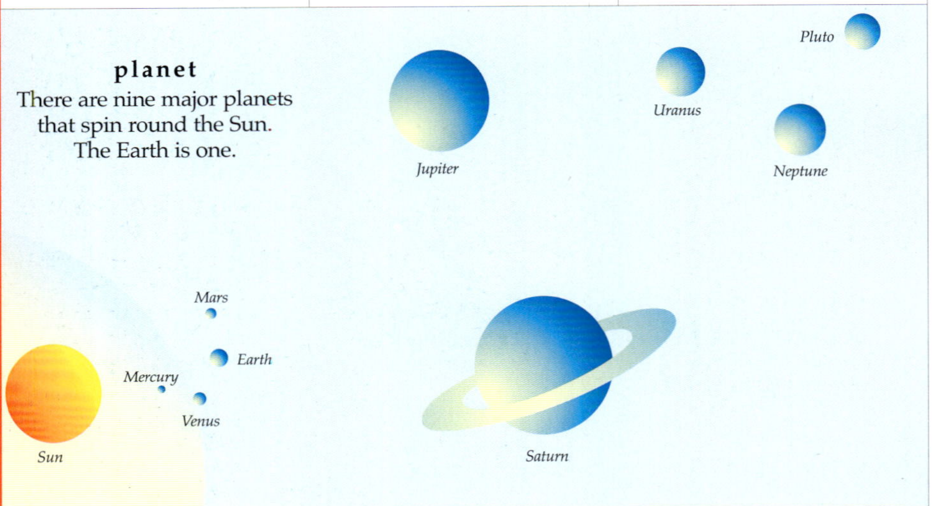

plant
A plant is a living thing which usually grows in soil. It also needs water, air and sunlight.

playground
A place for children to enjoy themselves. It is usually outdoors and might have swings, a slide or a climbing frame.

please
1. Ask nicely - if you say "please" politely then you can have another ride on my bicycle!
2. My aunt is very pleased with me. I have made her happy.

plastic
A man-made material which can be pressed and moulded into many shapes.

plus
Two plus two equals four. Plus means to add to.

poem
A poem describes something, usually in rhyme. Can you write poetry?

point
1. The sharp end of a thing.
2. It's very rude to point.

poison
A harmful or fatal substance.

police
People who are trained to keep law and order.

pollute
To make the Earth dirty and dangerous by getting rid of waste carelessly.

pond
A pool of water full of interesting wildlife in the water or around its edge.

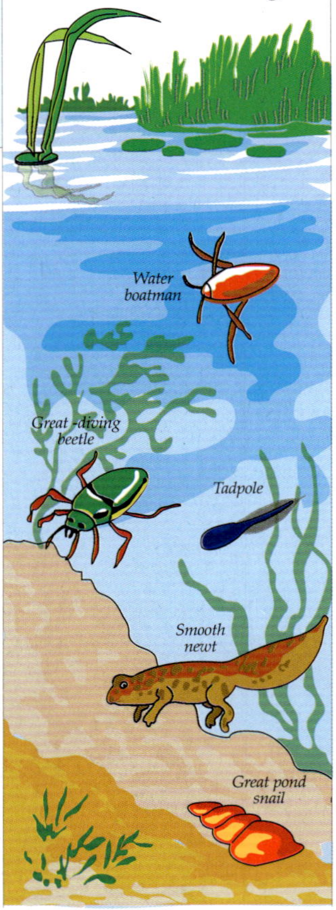

poor
If you are poor you have very little money or possessions.

population
The number of people that live in one particular place.

porridge
Do you eat porridge for your breakfast?

possible
If a thing is possible, it can be done.

poster
Someone has stuck posters all over this wall.

postman
A person who collects and delivers letters and parcels.

pour
You pour liquid out of one container into something else.

powder
Powder is like dust, very fine and light.

powerful
Powerful means very strong. That engine looks really powerful.

praise
When you praise a person, you tell them they have done well. Congratulations!

prepare
The chef prepared the pizza He got it ready.

present
A present is a gift to give or to receive.

pretend
When you pretend, you make-believe. Lucy is pretending she is grown-up.

pretty
Doesn't this little girl look pretty. She thinks she does too!

price
What price is that melon? How much money do I need to buy it?

prince
The son of a king or queen.

princess
The daughter of a king or queen.

print
A print is an impression or mark, like a fingerprint or footprint.

printing
Printing words and pictures in a book or newspaper is done on a printing machine. Letters covered in ink are pressed or printed onto paper.

prize
A reward for winning. This little pig has won first prize.

problems
Problems are always difficult to solve.

programme
1. What is your favourite programme on television?
2. Paul collects football match programmes, Sophie saves them from the theatre.

promise
To give your word and keep it. Dad promised we could go to the zoo.

protect
All animals and birds protect their young. They shield them from danger and harm.

proud
Mother was very proud on sports day when Dad won the parents' race.

prove
To prove is to show something can be done or that it is true.

pudding
A pudding is the sweet tasting part of a meal.

puddle
A small pool of water outside in the road or inside on the floor.

pull
The tug-of-war team pulled hard on the rope. Each side is trying to make the rope come towards them.

pump
When your tyres are flat, you use a pump to force air into them.

punch
To punch is to hit hard with your fists. Boxers punch with their gloves on.

pupil
Here are some pupils from Dinglewood School learning their lessons!

puppet
Puppets are dolls that move if somebody else pulls the strings.

purse
A purse is a small bag to keep your money safe.

push
When you push, you press against something until it moves.

puzzle
A puzzle is difficult to solve or understand.

pyjamas
I see you are wearing your pyjamas. You must be ready for bed!

Q q

queen
A woman who rules a country or the wife of a king.

question
You ask a question to find out something. What is on the blackboard? The answer to that question is, a question mark!

quack
When ducks make a noise, they quack.

queue
A line of people or vehicles waiting their turn.

quarrel
If you quarrel with someone, you get angry and argue.

quick
Quick means fast or speedy. Be quick! Then you will win the rally.

quarter
Cut a thing into four equal parts and you have four quarters. One of the parts is a quarter.

quilt
A padded cover for a bed. Here is a patch-work quilt.

quiz
A quiz is like a test, but is a bit more light-hearted. You must answer a number of questions.

R r

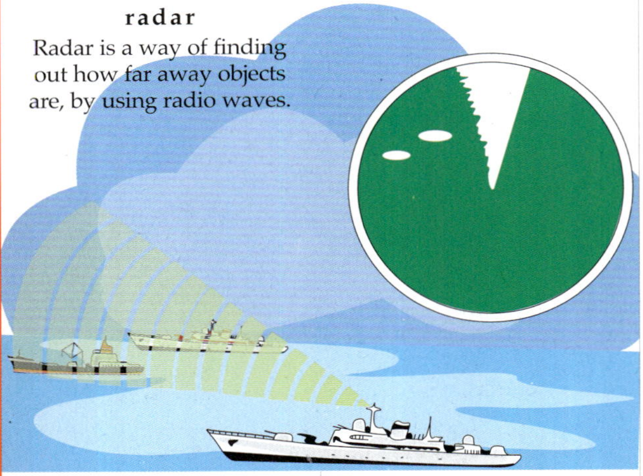

radar
Radar is a way of finding out how far away objects are, by using radio waves.

raft
A raft is a floating platform, sometimes made of logs lashed together.

rain
When it rains, water drops from clouds in the sky and falls down to Earth.

rainbow
Rainbows are caused by sunlight shining through raindrops. A rainbow is split up into seven colours.

rare
Something rare is uncommon. There are not many of them.

raw
Raw meat and vegetables are not cooked.

ray
Rays from a lamp are beams of light. Sunbeams are thin rays of sunlight.

razor
Father shaves with a razor. It has a very sharp blade.

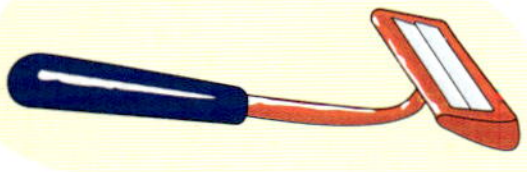

reach
1. To reach is to stretch towards something.
2. We have reached the sea at last. We have got there.

read
You look at words and understand them.

ready
Are you ready to go camping? Are you prepared with all you need?

real
This is not a real man, it's a toy. The little boy is just pretending he's real.

receive
To receive something is to be given it.

recipe
A recipe tells you how to make a dish and what to put in it.

recite
When you recite a poem, you say it out loud.

record
1. Put a record on the record player and dance to the music.
2. This pole-vaulter has just set a new world record.

referee
A referee makes sure the players keep to the rules of the game.

refrigerator
An ice-cold cupboard that keeps food fresh and cool.

remain
Father remained to fix the leak. He stayed behind and we left!

remember
To keep something in your mind and not forget. Remember the steep hill!

remind
When you remind someone you jog their memory. Did you remember to water my plant?

remove
Remove your muddy shoes. Take them off!

repair
Broken things must be repaired.

reply
To reply is to answer. "Who are you?" asked Alice. "The White Rabbit," he replied.

reporter
A reporter interviewed us today. Perhaps we shall be on television or in the newspapers tomorrow.

reptile
A cold blooded creature with a scaly skin.

rescue
If you save a person from danger you rescue them.

rest
1. When you feel tired, sit down and rest.
2. Leave the washing-up. I will do the rest of it later.

restaurant
Meals are served in a restaurant. You get a bill when you have finished.

return
1. When John returned my model, it was broken.
2. Swallows come to Britain in March and return to Africa in September.

reward
A reward is like a prize. You might get a reward for finding something.

rhyme
1. Words sounding the same.
2. Rhymes are small poems like nursery rhymes.

rhythm
Shake a tambourine in time to the music and you've got rhythm.

rice
Rice is a grain like grass. It grows in fields flooded with water.

ride
To be carried along by a machine or an animal.

right
1. Right is opposite to left.
2. Am I right in thinking you come from Australia?

ring
1. A ring fits your finger.
2. A ring can be a circle shape.
3. Bells ring ding-a-dong!

rink
A very large area with plenty of room for ice-skating or roller skating.

ripe
When fruit is ripe, it is ready to eat.

rise
Get up in the morning, rise and shine. The sun has risen in the sky.

roar
When lions and tigers make a noise, they roar.

river
Rivers begin in the hills as small streams. They grow deeper and wider then flow into the sea.

road
A road is a way on which people and vehicles travel.

rob
To rob is to steal. There's been a robbery at the bank, and the robber is getting away!

robe
Here is the mayor in his robes. Doesn't he look grand?

robot
A mechanical man. Andrew has a toy robot.

rock
1. Rock the baby's cradle from side to side.
2. A rock is a large stone. Rock climbing can be dangerous.

rocket
1. A firework on a stick.
2. Astronauts travel through space in a rocket.

roll
The wheel went rolling down the hill, it turned over and over.

roof
The roof covers the top of a building.

room
Rooms are different parts of a building or house

root
Dig up a plant, growing beneath the soil are the roots.

rope
A long thick twisted cord made up of lots of thin cords.

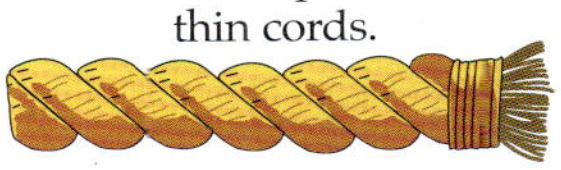

rough
1. The sea looks rough today.
2. What a rough hand you have, Mr. Gorilla.

round
A circle has a round shape and so has a ball.

row
1. These flowers are in a row.

2. Row a boat on the lake.

rub
To move and press one thing hard against another. Rub your shoes.

rubber
1. Rubber comes from the sap of a tree. Lots of things are made from it.
2. Jenny made a mistake in her drawing and rubbed it out with her rubber.

rubbish
Throw out all that rubbish! You don't need it any more.

rule
Orders that must be obeyed.

ruler
1. A ruler is a person who governs a country.
2. Use one to measure things.

run
Here are some runners running a race. How fast can you run?

rung
Climb up the ladder rung by rung.

S s

sad
Sally is sad, she is feeling very unhappy about something.

saddle
A seat on a bicycle or a horse.

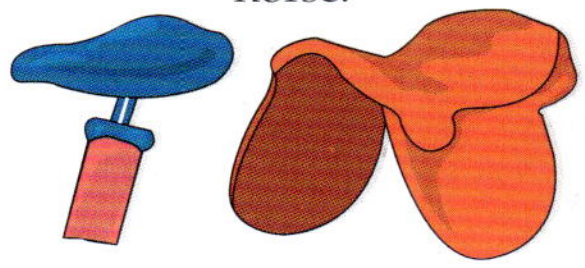

safe
Now he is safe, he is not in any danger.

sail
When the wind fills the sails the boat sails along. These sailors have sailed many a sea.

salad
Traditionally, vegetables or fruit eaten without cooking, although there are many fancy variations.

same
These twins look the same. They are alike except for the smudge on Gary's nose.

S s

sand
Grains of sand are made by rocks and shells ground down by the weather and sea.

sandal
An open shoe with straps.

sandwich
To make a sandwich you put your favourite food between two slices of bread.

sauce
Sauces add flavour to food.

save
1. When you save money you keep it to use later.
2. If you are a lifeguard you are trained to save lives.

scales
1. A weighing machine.
2. The hard flakes on the skin of fish and snakes.
3. Musical exercises.

school
Pupils go to school to learn. At the beginning they are taught to read and write.

science
In science we learn things by experiments, study and careful testing.

scissors
Scissors have two sharp blades fixed in the middle. They can cut paper, cloth and even your hair.

scooter
I can go really fast on my scooter!

scream
My mouse escaped and made my sister scream.

screw
A screw is like a nail with grooves, which fastens wood together. You use a screwdriver to turn a screw.

scroll
1. A roll of parchment or paper.
2. An ornamental shape
3. To move down a page with your eyes.

sculptor
A sculptor carves objects in stone and wood. They are called sculptures.

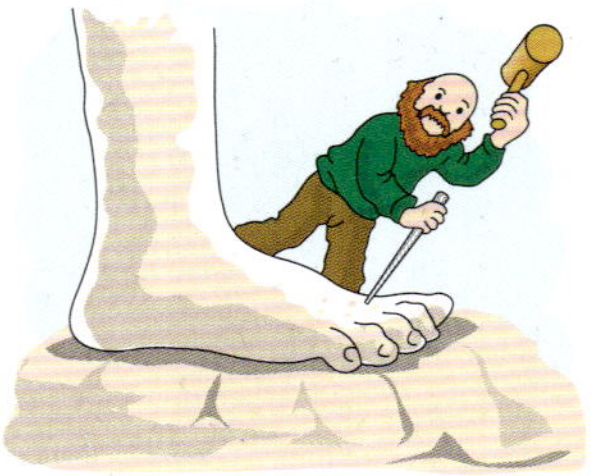

sea
Sea is salt water that covers a great part of our Earth.

search
When I searched for my tie, I looked everywhere.

season
There are four seasons, each one is a quarter of a year.

seaweed
Plants that grow in the sea.

secret
Something only one person knows, until they tell somebody else.

see
I can see you!
Can you see me?

seed
New plants grow from the seeds of the old plants.

sell
The greengrocer sells fruit. He sold me a pineapple.

see-saw
One side goes up, as the other side goes down.

self
When I'm by myself, I'm all alone. Myself is me.

send
Send Tim to fetch the coal. Make him go and get it.

sentence
I broke my leg and had to walk on crutches.
That sentence tells you in a few words a complete happening.

sentry
A soldier on guard. This soldier has a sentry box.

several
Several is more than one, perhaps two or three.

sew
A needle and thread and a piece of cloth is all you need to sew.

shadow
When the sun is shining, your shadow goes everywhere with you.

shake
To shake something you move it up and down or from side to side.

shallow
Shallow water is not deep.

shampoo
I get shampoo in my eyes every time Dad washes my hair!

shape
Everything and everybody has a different shape.

share
When I shared my grapes with Kim, I gave her part of them.

sharp
Don't play with knives. They are sharp and can cut you.

shed
A little hut outdoors for storing tools and all kinds of things.

sheet
1. Mother has the bed sheets hanging on the line.
2. Writing letters can use sheets and sheets of paper.

shelf
The shelf in my room was full up, so my Dad put up two more shelves.

shell
Eggs and nuts have a hard shell covering. So do some animals and sea creatures to protect themselves.

shelter
Shelter under my umbrella, it will protect you from the rain!

shine
1. If the sun shines it gives out a bright light.
2. When I have polished my shoes, they really shine.

ship
A large boat which can cross oceans.

shop
Different shops sell different things. What will you buy today?

short
Short is neither tall nor long. Which is the shortest pencil?

shorts
Doing sports we all wear shorts!

shout
People shout when they want to be heard.

shower
1. A shower is a quick sprinkling of rain.
2. Taking a shower on a hot day is very refreshing.

shrink
If you have a shower in your suit, it will shrink.

shut
When a thing is shut, it is closed; not open.

sick
I don't feel well today. I feel sick.

sign
A sign is a notice that tells you something.

silent
To be silent is to keep quiet.

silk
A fine thread spun by silkworms and woven into cloth.

silver
A precious metal that shines when polished.

similar
This book is similar to the other. It is almost the same.

simple
This game is simple, not difficult at all.

sing
You make music with your voice when you sing a song.

sink
1. The kitchen sink is full of dishes.

2. If your boat has a hole it will sink.

size
How big or how small you are is your size.

skeleton
All the bones in your body fit together and form your skeleton.

ski
Here is a skier skiing down a ski slope.

skin
Humans and animals have skin covering their body. Fruit and vegetables have skin too.

sky
The sky is up above you. It can be blue in the day, black at night, and sometimes grey and cloudy.

skyscraper
Skyscrapers are such high buildings, they seem to touch the sky.

sleep
Animals, birds and people, go to sleep to rest.

slice
To slice is to cut into flat thin pieces.

slow
Slugs and snails can't speed along, they always go slow!

small
Small is little; not big or tall.

smell
Some things smell lovely, some things smell terrible. Your nose tells you.

smile
You smile and look happy when you are pleased.

smoke
As a fire burns it gives off smoke.

smooth
A smooth thing has no bumps or sharp bits.

sneeze
When something tickles our nose, like pollen or dust, we sneeze.

snow
Tiny crystals of ice which form snowflakes then fall from the sky as snow.

soap
A good wash with soap and water makes the dirt disappear.

soft
Fur and feathers are soft to the touch, not hard at all.

soil
Plant a seed in the soil and watch it grow.

soldier
A soldier is a man in the army. These are soldiers from the past.

solve
To solve a puzzle or a mystery is to find the answer.

something
You never say what "something" actually is. I have something to show you!

sometime
At some time in the past or future.

sometimes
Occasionally. Sometimes we have a treat after our meal.

son
A son is the boy child of a mother and father.

song
A song is like a poem or rhyme set to music.

soon
I will go to bed soon, in a little while.

sorry
1. I felt sorry that the blackbird died. It made me feel sad.

2. Sorry I broke your vase. I do apologise.

sound
Every noise you hear is a sound.

soup
Soup is a liquid food with lots of flavour, made from meat and vegetables.

sour
Some fruits like gooseberries and rhubarb taste sour.

south
South is the point opposite to north. Countries with the word south in their name are usually hot.

space
A space is a place with nothing in it. There is no picture below, just a space.

speak
When you speak on the telephone you say something to the person at the other end.

special
Something special is not ordinary but different. Christmas is a special time.

speed
Speed is the rate you travel. High speed or low speed.

spell
1. Witches love casting evil spells.
2. To put the letters of a word in the right order.

spend
1. How much money will I have to spend to buy that?
2. I spend a lot of time at my Grandmother's house.

spill
When you knock over some liquid you spill it.

spin
1. A top spins when it turns round and round.
2. Spin on a spinning wheel and make a thread.
3. A spider spins to make a web.

splash
Jump into a pool. You will hear the splash as the water splashes out.

spot
A spot is a little mark. Spots are lots of little marks.

spread
When the baker spreads icing on a cake, he covers the top evenly.

spring
The first season of the year. Winter has passed and things start to grow.

square
A square has four corners and four straight sides of the same length.

squeeze
When you squeeze a lemon, you crush it or press it hard.

squint
When the eyes are turned in different directions you are squinting. If they are always like this, we say you have a squint.

stable
A building where horses are kept.

stairs
Steps for walking up and down to different levels of a building.

stamp
1. Stick a stamp on an envelope, then a rubber stamp will stamp the letter.

2. Do you ever stamp your foot in temper?

stand
Stand up, get on your feet! Don't sit there all day!

star
You can see stars at night as twinkling points of light in the dark sky. They are objects in space millions of kilometres away.

sport
Sport is a game or pastime.

start
To start a thing is to begin it. Start the race!

station
Travellers on trains and buses arrive and depart at the station.

stationary
When a vehicle or person has stopped and is no longer moving.

stationery
Writing paper, pens, pencils, erasers are all stationery, sold at the stationers.

stay
Stay where you are. Don't move from that spot!

steal
To steal is to take things that don't belong to you. The magpie stole the necklace!

steam
When water boils it turns into a misty cloud called steam.

steep
A hillside that is steep, slopes sharply.

step
Walk forward, back, and to the side, you are taking steps.

stick
1. Chop the logs into sticks.
2. Stick the paper on the wall.

sting
Bees and wasps have a sting in their tails.

stir
If you stir something with a spoon, you mix it up and move it round.

stitch
Push a needle and thread in and out of cloth and you have stitches.

stop
To stop is to cease what you are doing.

store
Animals store food for the winter. It is kept in a safe place until it is needed.

storm
Thunder, lightning, wind and rain all add up to a storm.

story
Tell a story about Aladdin. Is it true or made up?

straight
Draw a straight line with a ruler.

stranger
A stranger is someone you don't know. Don't talk to strangers!

stream
A little river of fresh running water.

street
A road with houses and shops on both sides.

stretch
If you stretch a thing it gets longer or wider. When you stretch you reach out.

stretcher
He was carried off to hospital on a stretcher.

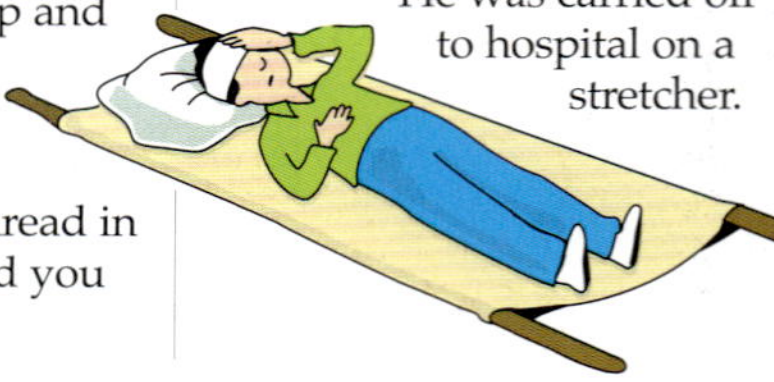

stripe
Stripes are lines of different colours.

strong
Strong is powerful. Look at this strong man lifting weights.

sum
When you add two or more numbers together, the total is the sum.

summer
The warmest season of the year. We hope it is hot on our summer holidays.

sun
The Sun gives us light and heat although it is about 93 million miles away.

sunburn
If we stay too long in the hot sun we go red and get painful sunburn.

supermarket
A huge store full of all kinds of food and other goods to buy.

surface
The top or outside of something.

surgery
You visit a surgery to see a doctor or dentist.

surname
Your surname is your family name.

surprise
If you don't expect something to happen, it comes as a surprise. Have you ever been to a surprise party?

surrender
The soldiers knew that they had to surrender because the enemy was far too powerful.

survive
To endure or live through something difficult. You cannot survive in the desert without water.

sweet
1. A pudding at the end of a meal.
2. This bag of sweets taste sweet.
3. This kitten looks so sweet.

swim
Everybody ought to learn to swim to be safe in the water.

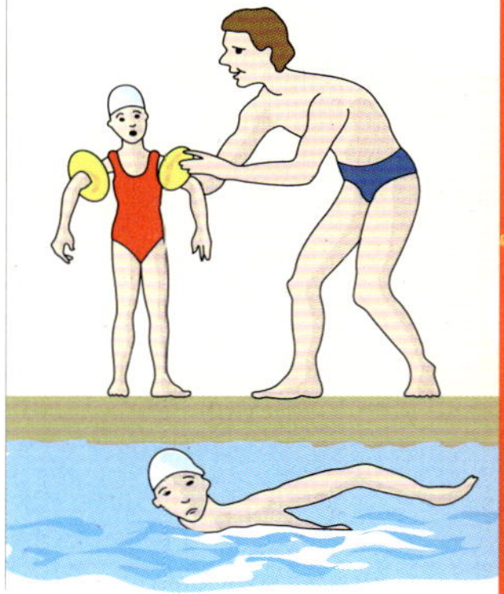

submarine
A boat that can sail on top of the water, then dive underneath and stay there.

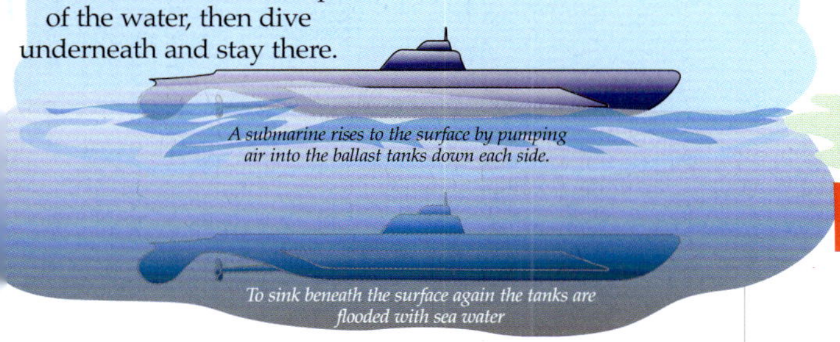

A submarine rises to the surface by pumping air into the ballast tanks down each side.

To sink beneath the surface again the tanks are flooded with sea water

subtract
Subtract is to take away.

sudden
All of a sudden an owl flew out of the tree. It happened unexpectedly.

sugar
Sugar makes things sweet. It comes from sugar cane and sugar beet.

suit
Is that your new suit? The trousers are too short and the jacket is too long!

supper
A snack to have at bedtime.

sure
I am sure my invitation said come in fancy dress. I am quite certain!

surf
Huge waves that crash onto the shore. Dare you ride the surf on a surfboard?

Tt

table
A piece of furniture with four legs and a flat top

tadpole
A tiny, black creature that wriggles out of frog-spawn, grows quickly and becomes a frog.

tail
A tail is the piece at the end. Animals' tails are at the end of their bodies.

take
When you take something you hold it with your hands. Sometimes you take things from one place to another, like taking the dog for a walk.

tall
Tall is high. A giraffe is tall but the trees are taller.

tame
Some animals are friendly and happy with people. They are tame not wild.

tap
1. To knock gently is to tap.
2. Turn off the kitchen tap!

tape recorder
A machine that can record sound on tape and play it back.

taste
We taste with our tongue, bitter, sweet or sour. When you eat a thing you taste it.

teacher
A teacher helps you to understand about many things. My teacher is teaching me all about Egypt.

team
A team is a group of people or animals working or playing together.

telephone
You can speak to someone far away on a telephone. Your voice is carried along wires to another phone.

telescope
When you look through a telescope you can see a long way, the lens makes things look bigger and nearer.

theatre
You go to see a play or show in a theatre.

there
"There" is somewhere else, it is not here. The balloon is over there. There it goes towards the mountain!

television
A television gives us pictures and sounds from signals sent through the air a long distance away. We need an aerial to receive them.

tell
"I must tell you what happened to me." Then Joe told us all about his accident.

temperature
How hot or cold something is. The instrument that measures temperature is a thermometer.

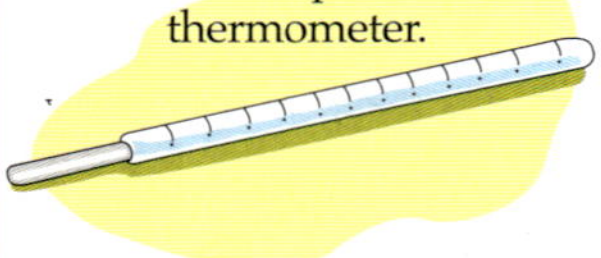

tent
A canvas shelter you can fold up and take anywhere.

terrible
Last night there was a terrible fire. It was dreadful and very frightening.

test
1. We are having a maths test to find out how much we know.
2. The man tested the hose and found it was working.

thank
If you are grateful for something, you say thank you.

thick
Wear a thick coat as the snow is very thick on the ground.

thin
Thin is opposite to thick. The oak tree trunk is thick, the silver birch is thin.

think
When you think, you are using your brains. Think about this problem.

thirsty
To be thirsty is to want a drink. Little children always feel thirsty in the middle of the night!

thousand
Ten hundreds are one thousand.

through
Through means from one side to the other. The builder knocked a hole through our wall!

throw
When you throw something you make it move through the air away from you.

ticket
A ticket shows how much you paid for something or to go somewhere.

tie
1. A tie is fastened round the neck in a knot or bow.
2. To tie a thing is to fasten it securely.

tight
This man's shirt is too tight. His buttons are popping off. It fits him too closely.

timber
Timber is wood which has been cut into pieces ready to use in building.

time
Time measures how long things take. What time did you leave school? Is it time to go yet?

tired
I'm so tired, I need a rest!

toboggan
A sledge turned up at the front for sliding down snowy slopes.

today
Today is this very day. It's Fred's birthday today!

together
Lucy and her cat play together every day. They are with each other all the time.

tomorrow
It is Saturday today. Tomorrow will be Sunday.

tonight
1. Tonight is the night after this day.
2. Mum is getting ready to go out tonight.

tool
There are lots of different tools that help us do our work.

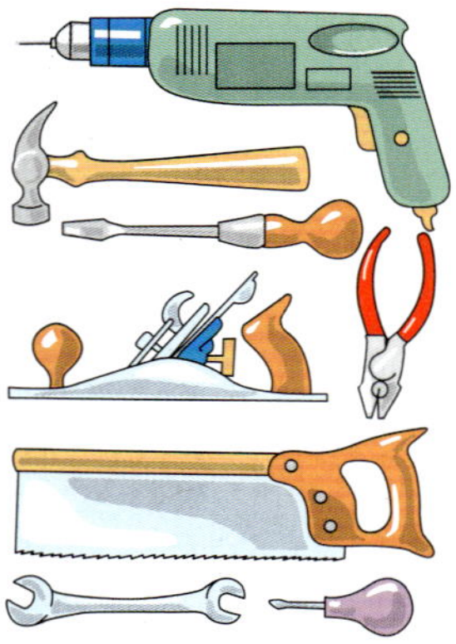

tooth
This baby has one tooth, soon he will have many more. You use your teeth to bite and chew. Look after them with a toothbrush and toothpaste.

top
The highest point of anything is the top.

torch
You can carry a torch in your hand, it gives a narrow beam to light your way in the dark.

touch
To touch is to feel with your hand. Wet paint, don't touch!

tough
Tough things are hard and don't break easily. My sister's rock cakes are tough!

towel
A soft, thick cloth for drying pots and people.

tower
A tall, high, narrow building or just part of one.

town
A town is full of people, streets, shops and houses. It is not as big as a city.

tractor
A tractor pulls farm machinery and moves heavy loads.

traffic
All vehicles that move are traffic, along the roads or in the air.

traffic lights
These lights control moving traffic at busy junctions and crossroads.

train
An engine pulling carriages or wagons along a track.

trampoline
Jump on the trampoline, see how high you can spring!

transparent
You can see right through things that are transparent.

trap
If an animal is caught in a trap it can't escape.

trapeze
Look at the girl swinging high up on the trapeze.

travel
To travel is to go from one place to another.

treasure
I think they have found buried treasure.

tree
A tree lives longer than any other plant. It has a trunk, branches and leaves.

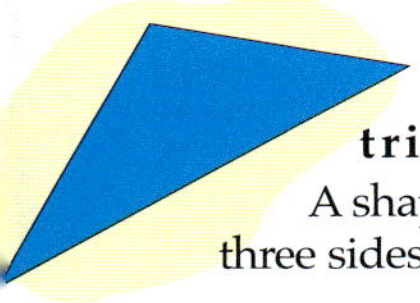

triangle
A shape with three sides joined.

trick
Can a magician really saw a lady in half, or is it a trick?

trolley
Do you ever ride in a supermarket trolley with the shopping?
Does your father use a golf trolley to carry his clubs?

trouble
If you upset a person or make things difficult, you are causing trouble.

truck
A truck is an open lorry for carrying goods.

true
Something that is true is certain and not a lie.
Is it true that chameleons change colour?

try
Try to climb to the top.
Do your best and try hard!

t-shirt
A vest with short sleeves shaped like a T.

tunnel
When a train goes into a tunnel it travels through a long dark passage cut through the ground.

turn
If something turns it goes round. Watch me turn a cartwheel!

typewriter
This office machine has lots of keys with a letter on each one. When they are pressed they print words on paper.

tyre
When the tyres of your bicycle are full of air, they help you ride along smoothly.

twin
A twin is one of two children born at the same time to one mother. Animals often have twins too.

U u

ugly
Cinderella's sisters were not pretty, they were Ugly Sisters.

umbrella
We open our umbrella to shield us from the rain, then close it when the rain stops.

uncle
The brother of your mother or father is your uncle.

under
Under means below.
What are you doing under the table?

understand
If you understand something you know what it means.

underwear
The clothes worn next to your skin.

undress
To take off your clothes.

unhappy
This little girl looks unhappy. I wonder why?

unicorn
A fairy tale animal with the body of a horse and a horn on its head.

uniform
Uniforms are the clothes of the same kind of people.

unique
One of a kind, different from every other one.
Each one of us is unique!

unite
We are united in our fight to save the whales from extinction. We are joined together as one.

unkind
The other birds were unkind to the Ugly Duckling. They were cruel and hurt his feelings.

untidy
Do you think this little boy is untidy?

unwell
My sister is unwell. She is feeling poorly and has to stay at home.

up
To go up is to rise. Up is the opposite of down.

upside-down
When you are upside-down, you are the wrong way up.

upstairs
Jane is climbing the stairs to bed. Her room is upstairs.

urgent
These medicines are very urgent. A patient needs them at once!

useful
Useful things are helpful. The red bucket is useful, just right for the job.

useless
Useless things are of no use at all. The blue bucket is quite useless because it is broken.

V v

vacant
This house is vacant. It is empty with nothing and nobody inside.

valley
The lower ground that lies between two hills.

van
A van is a covered truck with sides and a top. Have you ever moved house in a furniture van?

vanish
When things vanish, they disappear without a trace.

varnish
A paint which has a glossy finish. My sister is always varnishing her nails!

vase
You put flowers in a vase. Make sure they have some water.

vehicle
Anything that carries goods or people from place to place. Cars, lorries, buses, even wagons and carts are all vehicles.

vein
Blood returns to the heart for more oxygen through the veins in your body.

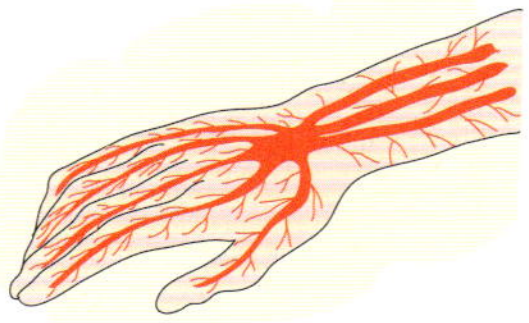

verb
Verbs tell of something being done. Swing, jump, laugh, play, are all verbs.

verse
"There was a bee
sat on a wall.
It said buzz
and that was all!"

vet
Vet is short for veterinary surgeon. A person who cares for sick animals.

viaduct
A road or railway bridge over a valley.

victory
When people or teams compete, one must lose and the other wins the victory.

view
This artist is painting the view. He is painting the landscape as far as he can see.

village
A village is much smaller than a town. It is in the country surrounded by farmland.

villain
A wicked person. We almost always have a villain and a hero in a pantomime.

vitamins
Vitamins help to make your body strong and healthy. They are found in many foods.

voice
You open your mouth and use your voice to speak.

volcano
A mountain that throws out red-hot lava, ash and gases through a hole in the top.

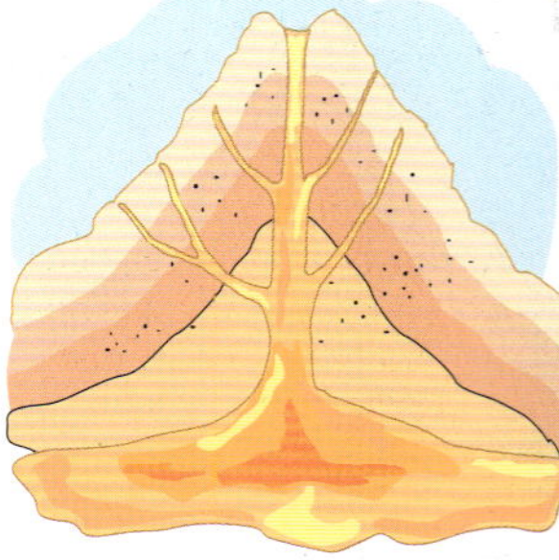

video recorder
A machine that records sounds and pictures on tape, then plays them back through your television.

video tape
A special tape for recording sounds and pictures in a video recorder.

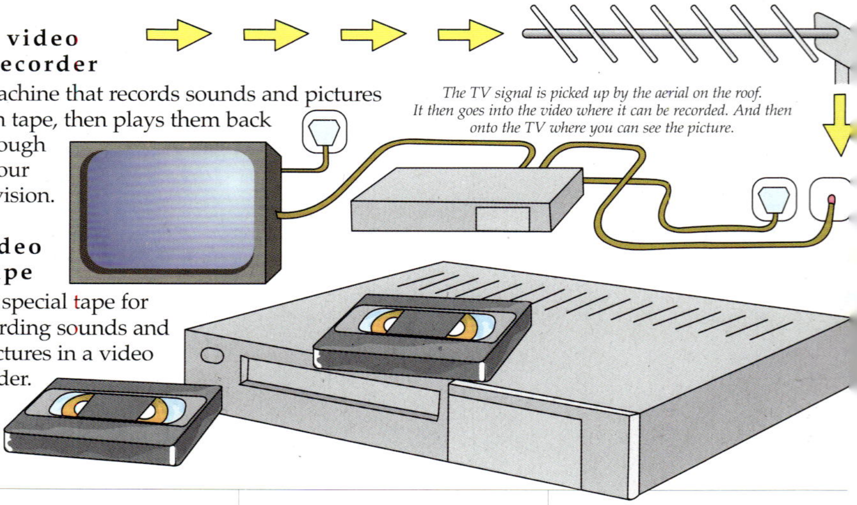

The TV signal is picked up by the aerial on the roof. It then goes into the video where it can be recorded. And then onto the TV where you can see the picture.

vegetable
A plant grown for food that is not a fruit.

violin
A musical instrument with four strings played with a bow.

visit
When someone calls to see you they pay you a visit. They are visitors.

vow
A solemn promise. Marriage vows are promises that a bride and groom make to one another.

vowels
The letters a, e, i, o, u are vowels.

voyage
A long journey far across the sea.

W w

wagon
Carts or trucks that can carry heavy loads from place to place by road or rail.

waist
You wear a belt round your waist. A waistcoat is a jacket without sleeves that just reaches your waist.

walk
We use our legs and feet to walk. We move along by putting one foot in front of the other.

wall
A boundary made of bricks or stones, also the side of a house.

want
This little girl wants her mother. She needs her and wishes she would come.

warm
Warm is between hot and cold. It's cold outside. Come and warm yourself by the fire!

warn
If someone is in danger and you tell them about it, you warn them.

wash
When we are dirty, water washes us clean. Most things come clean with water.

washing machine
A machine for washing lots of dirty clothes in a short time.

watch
1. You wear a watch on your wrist to tell you the time.
2. This boy is going to watch the match. He loves looking at football.

water
All living things need water to live. Water falls to Earth as rain, filling rivers, lakes and oceans.

watering can
We need water to drink and so do plants. When it is dry, water the flowers with a watering can.

wave
1. The Queen waved to me as she went by, and I waved my flag.
2. The surface of the sea moves up and down in waves.

way
1. How you do something is the way you do it. This is the way to stand on your head!
2. Do you know the way to the Moon?

wear
You wear clothes on your body. Dad is wearing his gardening clothes. The knees are worn out.

weather
Everybody talks about the weather. Is it wet or dry today? Will it rain, snow or blow?

weed
Gardeners think weeds are a nuisance, they pull them up because they are wild plants that they don't want in their garden.

week
A week has seven days. There are fifty-two weeks in a year.

weigh
If you weigh something you find out how heavy it is. How much do you weigh?

wheel
A wheel is a round shape that turns on its axle or centre. Wheels help things move more easily.

wheelbarrow
A little cart with one wheel in front and two handles and legs behind.

when
When will the train come? I shall lift your luggage aboard when you get on!

where
Where is my tie? It is where you left it.

which
Which watch has the second hand? Which asks what thing out of two or more things.

whisker
What a fine set of whiskers!

whisper
A whisper is a soft little voice. Whisper in my ear!

whole
Something that is whole is all there, nothing is missing. Mark said he could eat a whole French loaf!

why
"Why are you dressed like that?" When someone asks why, they want to know the reason.

"I am going to play American football!"

wicket
1. A small gate.
2. The set of three stumps and bails used in a match of cricket.

wide
This river is wide, it is broad not narrow.

wig
Artificial hair for the head.

wigwam
American Indians lived in tents called wigwams. They are made from poles covered in animal skins or tree bark.

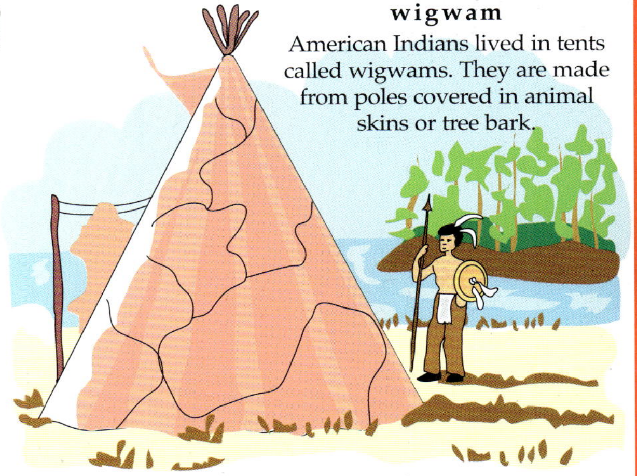

who
Who did that? Who threw that? Who broke that? "Who" asks "whatever" person.

wild
Animals that are wild are not tame. Wild plants grow in fields and hedgerows and not in a garden.

wind
The wind is air that is moving. Some winds are just a gentle breeze. See what a strong wind can do!

wind
To wind is to turn and twist. You wind up the clock by turning the key. Here is a road winding up a steep mountain side.

windmill
A mill that is driven by the force of the wind pushing the sails round. Windmills are used for grinding corn or pumping water.

window
A window in a building is made of glass to let in light. It can be opened to let in fresh air.

windscreen
A transparent shield in a vehicle to stop the wind and rain getting inside. It protects the passengers.

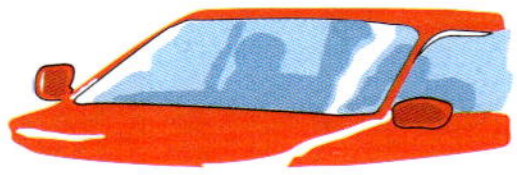

wing
Birds, insects and planes need wings to help them fly.

winter
The coldest season. Nights are long and dark and the days are short and cold with frost and snow.

wire
Wire is a thread made of metal. Different wires carry electricity and telephone messages to our houses.

wish
Make a wish! You really would like that wish to come true.

witch
Witches cast magic spells, but only in fairy stories!

wizard
A wizard is a man from legends and stories who can work magic.

woman
When a girl grows up she becomes a woman.

wood
1. A small group of trees, not as big as a forest, is called a wood.
2. Wood is a material that comes from trees. It is used in buildings and furniture and many other ways.

wool
The wool from sheep is spun into yarn then woven into cloth. Woollen clothes are warm and soft.

work
When anyone works they do a job. What work does this woman do?

world
Everything around us is our world. The Earth and sky is the world in which we live.

wrap
When it is cold mothers wrap up their babies tightly in covers before they go out.

write
When you write you put down words. You could write a few words, a letter, a story or a whole book.

wrong
Something wrong is not right or correct. Sarah has the wrong answer.

Xx Yy Zz

x-ray
Have you ever had a broken bone x-rayed? Invisible x-rays from a camera can pass through your flesh and take photographs which show doctors the inside of your body.

xylophone
A musical instrument made of pieces of wood or metal, each making a different note when hit by a hammer held in either hand.

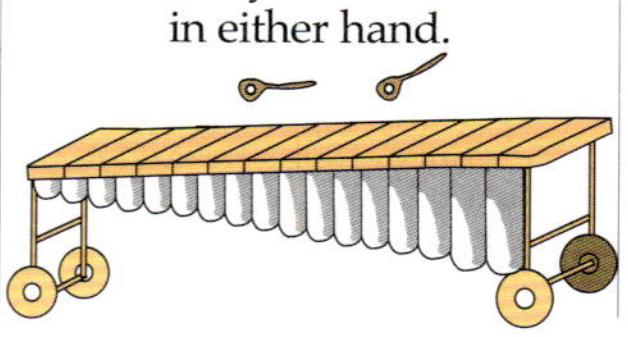

yacht
A yacht travels fast when the wind fills its sails.

yard
Yards are areas of hard ground outside houses and schools.

yawn
When you are tired or bored, you open your mouth wide and yawn.

year
This baby is one-year-old. She has lived 12 months or 52 weeks or 365 days.

yesterday
If today is Sunday, yesterday was Saturday.

yoga
My sister is practising her yoga. She is doing exercises and thinking.

yoghurt
A food made from milk which tastes thick and creamy. Which flavour do you like?

yolk
The yellow part of an egg.

young
When you are young, you are not grown-up. Everyone was young once!

your
Something that is yours belongs to you. I know this is your notebook. It has your name all over it.

youth
1. A young lad.
2. The time when you are young.

zebra
A zebra is an African wild horse with stripes.

zero
Zero is nothing, none, 0.

zigzag
A line with sharp angles. If you travel in a zigzag you move suddenly from side to side.

zip
A zip has two sets of metal or plastic teeth that grip each other and fasten things together.

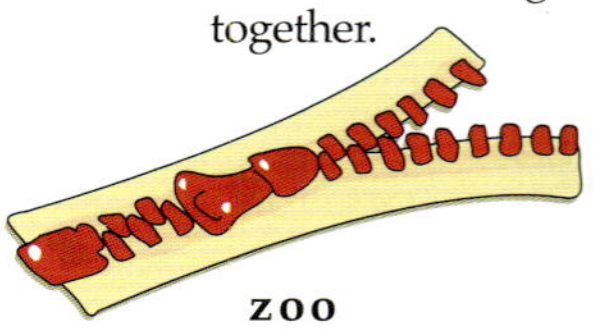

zoo
A zoo is the place to see all kinds of different animals. Most of the animals are kept in enclosures or cages.

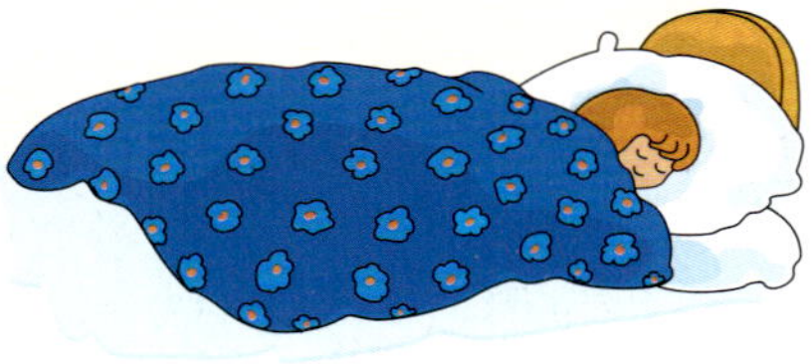